# The Indoor Grill Cookbook

*An Indoor Grill Guide
with More Than 100
Delicious and Healthy
Recipes*

JED PARKS

# Table of Contents

# Introduction

Indoor grills permit you to whip up steaks, burgers, & grilled vegetables without leaving the kitchen. Indoor grills are recommended for anybody who does not have sufficient space for the outdoor grill. They might leave somewhat to be required in terms of smoky taste if that is what you are looking for, but they make for it with various other advantages. Advantages include compact & portable, improved heat distribution, simple to clean & maintain, more flexible, year-round usage even in rainy weather, more reasonable.

Because they are extra compact, indoor grills are usually the finest for cooking for only some people at a time, & many could also be utilized as a panini press or grill. For instance, a De'Longhi Livenza All-Day Grill would make you sincerely reconsider your demand for some other cooking appliance as you could manage it to make grilled sandwiches, waffles, & assorted BBQ things whenever you love, then put it away in a cupboard to free up the countertop space.

The grilling units usually use electric components to supply a continual heat source, although similarly, stovetop models are accessible in which the heat is provided by the stove. They might have a wide-open grill grate that the foodstuff is put on, or it might have a robust grooved grill. Indoor grills are generally often miniature tabletop models instead of a unit on the stand.

# Chapter 1: Introduction to Indoor Grilling

## What Is Meant By Grilling?

The scientific side explains grilling as dry heat, a fast-cooking method that operates a "substantial amount of immediate, radiant heat." Frying in a saucepan or grill uses conduction heating directly, whereas grilling is thermal radiation.

Grilling temps could frequently exceed 500°F/260°C making it a quick-cooking method that you should observe. If not, your perfectly grilled hot dogs will explode into road bursts in a few mins.

What really makes grilled meals taste well is the proteins browning & sugars, creating that lovely coloration & additional flavor profile on vegetables & meat. It is known as the Maillard reaction, & this browning occurs when foods reach temps over 155 °C/310 °F. When it happens to proper grilling, you cook food on the open wire grid and the fire directly above or beneath the food. Usually, if the heat source is directly above, it is known as broiling, although it still succeeds as grilling for our clarity.

## Grilling vs Barbeque

The disparity between grilling & barbecue is temp & cooking time. Grilling is rapidly cooking over high heat, whereas barbecue is gradually cooking over many hrs with minimal, indirect heat. You also usually need various equipment for every cooking method (though you could, surprisingly, smoke on grills & grill on certain smokers.) Another major difference between both cooking methods is the meat quality.

Meats that are fatty & tough need a lengthy slow cooking procedure to break through the collagen & other tissues to get the meat juicy & tender. That is why it is recommended to use bigger, more cheap cuts for barbecue. Alternatively, tender or lean meat, chicken, & seafood need quick cooking over high temp to bring the inner temp up to a secure level without drying it out.

## How to Discover the Top Indoor Grill?

Before purchasing the indoor grill, think about these things:

### Size

For 1 to 2 individuals, an 80 square inches area is perfect. A 100-150 square inches area could feed 3 to 5 individuals. You would have to grill in batches for bigger groups because indoor grill ranges cap at around 150 sq inches.

### Versatility

Some grills open flat & let you swap out a grill with the waffle plate or griddle. Anything that gets removable plates which are dish washer safe, makes clean a breeze.

### Heat

Specific models do not let you adjust a cooking temp, while some others are changeable within reach. If you need a nice sear on your burgers or steak, be sure that it turns up to 500°F.

Here are the top indoor grills you could purchase in 2021

## 1. Griddler Five

This highly rated & trendy Cuisinart indoor grill could do it all. Experts discovered the digital mechanisms simple to use & appreciated setting a specific temperature for more accurate cooking, not like many other editions. Even improved. The plates are dishwasher-secure for fast clean-up.

It also changes to a griddle (8 pancakes can be cooked at one time), and you can purchase waffle plates. It is recommended to place parchment paper or foil beneath the back legs for less disarray since the topmost plate could drip while cooking greasy foods.

- Accurate temp control
- Dishwasher-secure grill plates
- Changes to a griddle

## 2. Steak Lover's Grill (Indoor)

As its name indicates, this model is the ultimate purchase for anybody who likes steaks with picture-ideal grill features. In the Lab tests, it made fantastic marks contrasted to other grills — at a portion of the price. The digital temp control with a ninety-second sear function is also great. Remember: The plates are not removable, so it is recommended to use a wet towel while it is warm to release any stuck-on excess.

- Inexpensive
- Digital temp control
- Hard to clean

## 3. Contact Smokeless Grill

Great for anybody with storage space or a limited counter, this George Foreman could be stored side when you are not using it. These grills have done solidly in all the cooking evaluations, draining grease properly & smooth of cleaning credits to dishwasher-reliable plates. The lowest plate on this edition has higher trims that help make a firm seal for quick cooking & drain holes built perfectly to help with cleanup & smoky smells.

- Stores upright for tiny spaces
- Simple to clean
- Rapidly cooking

# Chapter 2: Stove Top Grill Recipes

## Chops Cajun pork

Preparation Time: 17 Mins

Servings: 6

### Ingredients

- One tsp garlic powder
- 3⁄4 tsp white pepper
- One tbsp paprika
- One tsp onion powder
- 3⁄4 tsp black pepper
- 1⁄2 tsp ground red pepper
- Six center-cut, pork chops (around 2-1/2 lbs. total)
- 3⁄4 tsp dried thyme
- 3⁄4 tsp dried oregano

### Instructions

1. Preheat grill to a medium-high temperature. Add all the ingredients in a small bowl, excluding the pork chops, and blend well. Rub spice combination above

the pork chops, rubbing well on all sides.

2. Grill pork chops for five-six minutes on each side or until cooked to your desired.

# Lemonade salmon (Grilled)

Preparation Time: 1hr 40 mins

Servings: 4

## Ingredients

- Two tbsps. olive oil, as well extra for drizzling
- Two tsps. Chopped fresh ginger.
- One cup lemonade
- 1/4 cup, soy sauce
- One lemon juice & zest of, additional one lemon & cut it in thin rounds.
- Fresh ground black pepper & kosher salt
- Two tbsps. brown sugar
- Two garlic cloves, chopped.
- 1/4 cup, chopped fresh parsley.
- 1 1/2 lbs., salmon fillets with the skin on, cut in the middle.
- One red onion & cut into half-inch-thick rounds.

## Instructions

1. Whisk together olive oil, ginger, lemonade, soy sauce, lemon zest, 1/2 teaspoon salt, brown sugar, garlic, and 1/4 teaspoon pepper in a medium mixing bowl.

2. Score the skin of salmon with the help of a sharp knife, creating three 1-inch incisions. Put the marinade over the onions and salmon in the baking dish. Refrigerate for one hour, turning halfway through.

3. Drain the remaining liquid after removing the onions and salmon from the marinade. Drizzle olive oil into a nonstick grill pan on medium heat. Put the salmon skin-side down on the pan. Arrange the lemon slices and onion rounds on all sides of the fish in the pan.

4. Cook for another three to five minutes before flipping the fish, lemons, and onions, five to eight minutes on the grill, till the salmon, is cooked all through & the onions are lightly charred and soft.

5. Arrange the salmon on a serving platter. Season with pepper and salt and garnish with lemon slices, lemon juice, grilled onions, and parsley.

# Lemon, garlic, and ginger swordfish steak.

Preparation Time: 31mins

Servings: 4

## Ingredients

- One lemon juice
- Two tbsps. olive oil
- Four swordfish steaks
- Two spring onions are finely chopped.
- 2 1/2 cm, gingerroot, peeled & wonderfully chopped.
- Two garlic cloves & crushed.
- One red chile, deseeded & finely chopped.

## Instructions

1. In a small bowl, combine the garlic and ginger to make a paste. Mix in the chili, lemon juice, spring onions, and oil until all is well mixed.

2. Add in the swordfish steaks and coat thoroughly. Allow 15 minutes for marinating.

3. Preheat the grill to a high temperature.

4. Put the fish on the grill rack after removing it from the marinade. 5-6 minutes before turning once.

5. Serve with lime wedges, mixed salad, and new potatoes. Drizzled with the residual marinade.

# Thai-style chicken thighs (grilled)

Preparation time: 25mins

Servings: 4

## Ingredients

- Twelve skinless & boneless chicken thighs
- 1/3 cup, chopped fresh basil.
- 1/3 cup, chopped fresh coriander (cilantro)
- 1 tbsp minced ginger
- 1 tbsp minced garlic
- 1 tbsp minced chili
- 1 1/2 tbsps. soy sauce
- 1 1/2 tbsps. fish sauce
- 1 1/2 tbsps. olive oil
- 1 1/2 tbsps. brown sugar

## Instructions

1. In a mixing bowl, mix all ingredients, excluding the chicken.

2. Combine all ingredients thoroughly.

3. Put the chicken and marinate for a minimum of an hour, ideally more.

4. Barbecue the chicken till golden brown & cooked through on the grill in the griller or hotplate.

5. Normally, twelve thigh fillets will feed four to six people.

# Grilled best pork chops

Preparation time: 2hrs 15mins

Servings: 6

## Ingredients

- 1/4 cup, vegetable oil
- Three tbsps. seasoning of lemon pepper
- Half cup of water
- 1/3 cup, light soy sauce
- Two garlic cloves, chopped.
- Six pork loin chops & fat eradicated

## Instructions

1. Combine all marinade ingredients in a large mixing bowl.
2. Leave to marinate for a minimum of 2 hours.
3. Eradicate from marinade and cook for 15 minutes or until finished on a greased grill over medium-high heat. Cooking time for the second side is for 1-2 minutes less. 3/4"/thinner, maximum five-six minutes each side; thicker than 3/4", maximum 6-7 minutes per side.
4. Do not over the grill; otherwise, the chops will turn out to be tough. Rotate chops forty-five degrees after two minutes on either side of the grill for even cooking. When juices collect on the top surface & the meat seems to be halfway cooked, flip it.

# Garlic grilled pork tenderloin

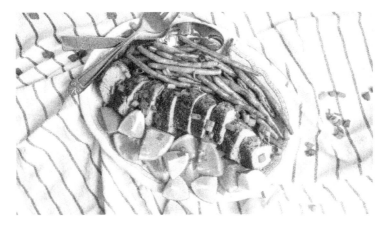

Preparation time: 24hrs 15mins

Servings: 6

## Ingredients

- Two tbsps. Grated fresh ginger root.

- Two tsps. Dijon mustard

- Six garlic cloves, chopped.

- Two tbsps. soy sauce

- 1/3 cup, fresh lime juice

- Four (3/4 lb.) pork tenderloin & trimmed.

- Half cup, olive oil

- cayenne (taste)

## Instructions

1. In a food processor or blender, combine all ingredients, excluding the pork, and season with pepper and salt to taste.

2. Mix it.

3. Put the marinade over the pork in a resealable plastic container.

4. Refrigerate for one-two days, turning occasionally.

5. Allow 30 minutes for the pork to come to room temperature before cooking.

6. Cook over a preheated grill, turning every five minutes, till a meat thermometer reads 160 degrees (around fifteen-twenty minutes).

7. Allow cooling for 5 minutes before slicing.

# Pan pork chops (grilled)

Preparation time: 46mins

Servings: 4

## Ingredients

- One tsp dried thyme
- Half tsp freshly ground pepper
- Four pork chops, half to one inch thick
- One tsp salt
- One-two tbsp oil

## Instructions

1. Season the chops of pork with salt, pepper, and thyme.

2. Set aside for 30 mins. on the counter.

3. Heat the oil in a big stainless-steel skillet over medium heat.

4. Arrange the chops in the pan in such a way that they do not strike.

5. Cook each surface gradually (on a lower heat setting if required) until golden brown.

6. Each side will take around 4 mins.

7. Put a tight-fitting lid on the pan.

8. Remove the chops from the heat and set them aside for 8 -10 mins, contingent on their thickness.

9. Finally, deglaze a pan by using slight water, broth, or wine and a dip of butter once removing the chops, and then serve it as a sauce.

# Moroccan grilled chicken

Preparation time: 42mins

Servings: 4

## Ingredients

- Four skinless & boneless chicken breasts
- 1/4 cup minced parsley
- 1/4 cup, minced fresh cilantro.
- Half cup olive oil (extra virgin)
- 1/4 cup, scallion chopped (only white part)
- Two tsps. ground cumin
- One tsp salt
- One tbsp chopped garlic
- Two tsps. paprika
- 1/4 tsp, turmeric
- 1/4 tsp, cayenne pepper

## Instructions

1. In a food processor container, combine the parsley, oil, scallions, garlic, cumin, cilantro, cayenne pepper, paprika, salt, turmeric, and salt.
2. Blend until entirely smooth.

3. Rub the chicken breasts on both sides with the mixture and set aside for 30 minutes.

4. Preheat the barbecue grill to a medium-high setting.

5. Cook the chicken breasts for approximately 6 mins on each surface or till cooked through.

# Flank marinated steak

Preparation time: 2 hrs. 15 mins

Servings: 4

## Ingredients

## Marinade

- 1/4 cup, canola oil

- 1/4 cup, teriyaki sauce or 1/4 cup, teriyaki marinade

- 1/4 cup, honey

- One tsp ginger root, minced.

- Half cup, soy sauce

- Four garlic cloves, minced.

## Steak

- One lb. flank steak

## Instructions

1. In a big zip loc container, mix all the marinade ingredients.

2. Make shallow diagonal cuts around the steak to score it.

3. Put the steak in the bag and seal it.

4. Refrigerate for a minimum of 2 hours before serving (up to twenty-four hours).

5. Remove the steak from the bag when prepared to cook.

6. You have the choice of grilling or broiling it.

7. Cook for 12 to 14 minutes, or till target doneness is achieved (One hundred- and sixty degrees F for medium doneness).

8. If you would like to serve the marinade as a sauce, heat it in a small size saucepan to a boil, then turn off the heat.

# Secret steak of sirloin

Preparation time: 2hrs 35mins

Servings: 4-6

## Ingredients

- 1/4 cup, Perrins & Lea Worcestershire Sauce, additional
- One tsp Perrins & Lea Worcestershire Sauce, separated
- Two tbsps. Lemon juice or two tbsps. lime juice
- Two tbsps. olive oil
- 1/4 cup, immediately chopped onion.
- 3/4 tsp salt
- Half tsp instant chopped garlic
- Three lbs. sirloin steaks
- Two tbsps. Butter or Two tbsps. margarine
- One tbsp chopped parsley

## Instructions

1. Toss together 1/4 cup of Perrins® & Lea, oil, minced onion, lemon juice, salt & chopped garlic; set aside.

2. Put the steak in a plastic bag or a bowl of tight-fitting.

3. Drizzle the Lea& Perrins® combination over the steak.

4. Leave to marinate for a minimum of 2 hours.

5. Take the steak out of the marinade.

6. Arrange on a rack.

7. Cook for 7 to 10 minutes on every side on hot charcoal or under a preheated hot broiler until cooked to your desired, brushing with leftover marinade if needed.

8. Put the steak on a serving tray.

9. Melt butter in a small size saucepan.

10. Add the remaining 1 tsp Perrins® & Lea and parsley.

11. Put the sauce over the steak.

# Grilled fish in foil sliced acods

Preparation time: 17mins

Servings: 4

## Ingredients

- 1/4 cup, lemon juice
- One tbsp chopped fresh parsley.
- 1/4 tsp freshly ground black pepper.
- 1/4 tsp paprika
- One tsp salt
- One onion & thinly sliced.

## Instructions

1. Cut large squares of thick aluminum foil. On every piece of foil, evenly distribute the fish fillets.

2. Melt butter in the saucepan. Combine the parsley, salt, lemon juice, and pepper in a mixing bowl.

3. Combine all ingredients in a large mixing bowl and stir well. Pour the sauce over the fish, then top with onion slices and paprika.

4. Fold and close the foil around the fish & seal it.

5. Grill for five to seven minutes on each side of the grill. When the fish is cooked, it can flake quickly. And then serve.

# Garlic honey pork chops (grilled)

Preparation time: 25mins

Servings: 6

## Ingredients

- 1/4 cup, soy sauce
- 1 1/2 lbs. (6 4 oz. portions) boneless, pork chops
- Two garlic cloves, chopped.
- One cup ketchup
- 1/3 cup, honey
- Pepper & salt

## Instructions

1. Combine the ketchup, garlic, honey, and soy sauce in a mixing bowl.

2. Place aside.

3. Season pork lightly with pepper and salt.

4. Using a pastry brush, cover each chop in a sauce.

5. Cook chops for around 5 minutes on each side or till meat is cooked all through on a greased grill four to six inches (ten to fifteen cm) from medium-set or medium-hot coal, basting with a sauce frequently.

# Catfish Cajun-style (grilled)

Preparation time: 15mins

Servings: 4

## Ingredients

- One tsp creole seasoning
- One tsp blackened fish for seasoning
- One tsp lemon pepper for seasoning
- One tsp white pepper
- lemon wedge, for garnish
- Four catfish fillets, 1 1/2 to 2 lbs.
- Two tbsps. lemon juice

## Instructions

1. Mix the first four ingredients and rub the seasoning on the catfish. Lemon juice should be applied to each side of the fish.

2. Cook for 5 minutes on all sides on medium-hot coals (minimum 350-400°F), covered with a grill cap, till fish flakes easily with a fork. If needed, serve with a squeeze of lemon.

# Hamburgers

Preparation time: 20mins

Servings: 3-4

## Ingredients

- Two garlic cloves
- 1/4 tsp salt
- One lb. lean ground beef
- One tbsp olive oil
- One tbsp horseradish (optional)
- Two-three tbsps. Worcestershire sauce

## Instructions

1. Peel and chop the garlic cloves on a wooden surface before placing them in a pestle and mortar.

2. Make a paste with olive oil and salt.

3. Combine the meat, Worcestershire sauce, and horseradish in a mixing bowl.

4. Combine all ingredients in a mixing bowl and change seasonings to taste.

5. For making patties, use your thumb to put an indentation in the middle of every single one (nearly the way all through). The burgers would not shrink because of this.

6. When finished, season with pepper and salt to taste.

# Chicken grilled wings

Preparation time: 35mins

Servings: 6

## Ingredients

- Two tsps. olive oil
- Four garlic cloves, chopped.
- Three lbs. chicken wings
- Half cup Dijon mustard
- 1/4 cup, soy sauce
- Half tsp ground ginger

## Instructions

1. Remove the tips from the chicken wings and cut them into three pieces.

2. In a mixing bowl, combine the remaining ingredients.

3. Stir in the wings.

4. Cover and set aside for forty-five minutes to marinate.

5. Brush the remaining mixture on the pieces and put them on the grill.

6. Cook for 15-20 minutes on medium-hot coals, turning once.

# Caribbean simple jerk chicken

Preparation time: 1hr 45mins

Servings: 6

## Ingredients

- Two tbsps. oil
- Two tbsps. soy sauce
- One packet Italian salad mix dressing
- Two tbsps. brown sugar
- Half tsp ground red pepper
- 2 1/2 lbs. pieces of chicken
- One tsp cinnamon
- One tsp thyme

## Instructions

1. In a mixing bowl, combine all ingredients, excluding the chicken.

2. Put it on the chicken.

3. Cover & marinate for a minimum of one hour or all night in the fridge.

4. Cook it on the grill. Enjoy.

# Tuna grilled steak

Preparation time: 55mins

Servings: 4

## Ingredients

- Two tsps lime juice
- Two tsps lemon juice
- 1/4 cup, olive oil
- Four tsps Old Bay Seasoning
- One lb. tuna steak

## Instructions

1. Whisk together the Old Bay, olive oil, lime juice, and lemon juice.
2. Combine well.
3. Put it on the Tuna steaks & marinate for a minimum of twenty minutes, turning infrequently.
4. Preheat the grill to high heat & sear the steaks for one to two minutes on each side to seal in juices.
5. Finish the cooking eight to ten minutes per inch of the thickness, somewhat away from the hottest place.

# Crab grilled legs

Preparation time: 16mins

Servings: 4

## Ingredients

- 2 tbsps. olive oil
- Three-four lbs. legs of king crab or three-four lbs. Dungeness crab legs, cooked

## Instructions

1. Heat the grill.
2. Brush each side of the crab legs with the oil & place it on a hot grill five to six from coals. Heat for a minimum of 4 to 5 minutes before turning once.
3. Remove to the plates & serve with a dipping sauce of your desire.
4. A good dipping sauce is garlic butter sauce, red cocktail sauce, or a thinned down guacamole dip. You can also squeeze the fresh lemon on tuna before eating it.

# Easy baked BBQ chicken

Preparation time: 50mins

Servings: 4

## Ingredients

- 1/4 cup, A.1. Original Sauce
- Four chicken thighs
- One cup of barbecue sauce

## Instructions

1. Preheat the oven to approximately 425 degrees Fahrenheit.
2. Combine A1 and BBQ Sauce in a mixing bowl.
3. Drizzle the sauce mixture over the chicken.
4. Bake over 40 mins, often basting with sauce unless all of it is gone.

# Grilled spicy fish

Preparation time: 15mins

Servings: 4

## Ingredients

- 1/4 cup, vegetable oil
- One tsp paprika
- Half tsp cayenne pepper, according to taste
- Two tbsps. low-level sodium soy sauce
- Twenty-four ounces of catfish fillets or twenty-four ounces of other mild fish
- 1/4 cup, lemon juice
- Three green onions, minced, white & green parts.
- One tsp onion powder
- Two tbsps. Fresh ginger is perfectly chopped or two tsps. Ground ginger.
- Six garlic cloves, perfectly chopped, around one tbsp.

## Garnish

- parsley, minced (if needed)
- lemon wedge (if needed)

## Instructions

1. In a large mixing bowl, combine the ginger, minced onion, green onions, garlic, lemon juice, cayenne pepper, soya sauce, paprika, and vegetable oil.
2. Put the fish in a zip-top bag with the liquid mixture and seal the bag. After sealing and marinating, refrigerate it for 1-2 hrs.
3. Lightly oil the grill grate and preheat the grill to moderate-high. Cook the fish for about 4 mins on either side of the grill. Just toss the fish once and rub it with the remained marinade.
4. NOTE: Fish is fully cooked once the color changes from transparent to white or when the internal temperature reaches 150 degrees Fahrenheit. Avoid overcooking fish to the point that it "flakes," indicating that it has become dry.

# Flat grilled iron steak

Preparation time: 20mins

Servings: 6

## Ingredients

- 1 1/4 - 1 1/2 lbs., flat steaks
- Two garlic cloves crushed & peeled.
- One tsp Italian seasoning
- 1/4 cup, olive oil
- Two tbsps. balsamic vinegar
- Salt & black pepper

## Instructions

1. Place the steaks in a plastic bag that can be sealed.

2. Whisk together all the remaining ingredients in a small container. Pour the marinade on the steaks and let it sit for at least one hour to eight hours

3. Allow at least 60 mins for the meat to come to room temperature before grilling.

4. Remove the meat from the marinade and toss it out.

5. Put the steak on a hot grill and cook for 5 mins. Grill bridge marks can be reached by rotating the steak 45 degrees.

6. Flip the steak and switch it to a relatively cool section of the rack for another 4 mins of grilling. Take care not to overdo the food.

# Marinated best pork tenderloin.

Preparation time: 35mins

Servings: 12

## Ingredients

- Half garlic clove.
- One tsp shredded fresh ginger
- One cup, soy sauce
- Half cup, olive oil
- One tbsp brown sugar
- Three lbs. pork tenderloin

## Instructions

1. Place the pork tenderloin inside a big zip lock bag and seal it.
2. Peel the garlic cloves and gently crush them.
3. Place ginger and garlic in the bag.
4. In a medium mixing bowl, combine the olive oil, brown sugar, and soy sauce.
5. Pour the sauce over the pork tenderloin.
6.  Marinate for approximately three days in a zip lock bag in the refrigerator.
7.  Remove from the packet and discard the marinade.
8. Cook until medium on the grill or under the broiler in the oven (around 15 mins).
9.  Dark and delicious with a soft pink middle.
10. Serve over rice as well as with grilled asparagus and baked potatoes.

# Blackened Slammin salmon

Preparation time: 17mins

Servings: 2-4

## Ingredients

- Blackening seasoning
- Olive oil
- One lb. salmon fillet

## Instructions

1. Remove the salmon from the package & rub the skinless side with blackening seasoning.

2. Use just adequate to cover a piece of fish, not so much that pink underneath the seasoning is hidden.

3. Gently brush the grill pan with olive oil and heat on medium (lightly). Put the salmon skin on the side down in the pan & cook on medium heat till half of the salmon is opaque (from bottom-up).

4. Strip the skin from the salmon and flip it over. Cook for an additional 5-8 mins, or till the whole piece of the fish is opaque & runs with white milky substance (healthful omega fatty acids)

5. Serve instantly with potatoes or rice & a vegetable of your desire.

# Chicken kabobs & grilled steaks

Preparation time: 1hr 15mins

Servings: 6-8

## Ingredients

- Four tbsps. vegetable oil
- One yellow bell pepper & cut into one-inch pieces
- One green bell pepper & cut into one-inch pieces
- Three garlic cloves, minced.
- Three-four minced green onions
- One lb. Chuck steak & cut into one-inch pieces
- One lb. Chicken & cut into one-inch pieces
- 3/4 cup, dry sherry
- One tbsp fresh ginger
- Half cup, soy sauce
- One red bell pepper & cut into one-inch pieces
- One white onion & cut into one-inch pieces
- Skewer

## Instructions

1. In a 1-gallon zipper container, mix oil, garlic, sherry, soy sauce, green onion, and ginger.

2. Squish all together.

3. Add the meat, onion, and peppers to the pan.

4. Refrigerate for a minimum of one hour, preferably overnight.

5. Use metal ones or marinade bamboo skewers.

6. Heat the grill to med-high heat.

7. Skewer meat & vegetables alternately till all the ingredients are utilized up.

8. Put kabobs on the grill & cook till needed doneness is reached, turning on every 2 minutes.

9. The peppers & onions can stay tender and crisp. Your meat would the way overdone if you keep the kabobs on till the vegetables are soft. Make distinct kabobs for vegetables

and meat if you choose soft grilled vegetables. This will allow the vegetables to cook for longer.

10. Make different kabobs for beef & chicken, if you desired your beef a moderate rare. Be inventive.

# Mechel - marinated backstraps of lamb

Preparation time: 10mins

Servings: 6

## Ingredients

- One tbsp sweet paprika
- One tbsp lemon juice
- Two tbsps. olive oil
- Salt
- Two tbsps. minced garlic
- Two tbsps. minced coriander leaves
- One kg lamb backstrap
- One tbsp cumin
- Two tbsps. minced parsley (flat-leaf)

## Instructions

1. Put the lamb in a mixing bowl, combine the remaining ingredients, and mix well with your hands to coat the lamb thoroughly.

2. Set aside for a minimum of 1 hour in the refrigerator.

3. Cook on the grill until moderate-rare.

4. Don't forget to add the minted yogurt to the mix.

# Instantly grilled trout

Preparation time: 20mins

Servings: 4

## Ingredients

- Half tbsp freshly ground pepper
- One tbsp lemon juice
- Four rainbow trout
- One tbsp kosher salt
- Two tbsps. olive oil (extra virgin)

## Instructions

1. Cut the heads from the trout and clean them.

2. Preheat the grill to a high-searing temperature of about 400 degrees Fahrenheit.

3. Oil the exterior of the trout.

4. Season inside of the trout with pepper and salt.

5. If desired, squeeze some lemon juice over the trout.

6. Lower the heat to a medium (250 degrees) on the grill and put the trout on it.

7. Cook the trout quickly & must be flipped just as the grill side turns white.

8. The trout is done when all the meat is flaky and white (do not overcook it).

9. Instantly serve the trout.

# Grilled tilapia

Preparation time: 15mins

Servings: 4

## Ingredients

- One tsp Cajun seasoning
- Two lbs. tilapia fillets
- One tsp olive oil
- One tsp Old Bay Seasoning

## For the aioli

- 1 1/2 tbsps., Dijon mustard
- 3/4 tsp, dried tarragon
- One cup mayonnaise
- Six garlic cloves, minced.
- 1 1/2 tbsps., lemon juice

## Instructions

1. Preheat the grill to high.

2. Brush all sides of the fillets with oil.

3. Drizzle with the seasonings.

4. Cook for around 4 to 5 mins on moderately high heat on a hot grill. During the grilling process, turn once.

5. Serve it with aioli.

6. To make the aioli, add all ingredients to the bowl, whisk to combine, and chill till prepared to use.

7. To dip in aioli, you serve up with green beans and boiled new potatoes.

8. You can also use mayonnaise that is low in fat.

# Fish (grilled) with butter sauce, garlic, and white wine

Preparation time: 1hr

Servings: 2

## Ingredients

## Sauce

- Two garlic cloves, finely chopped & crushed.

- 1/4 cup, unsalted butter at a room temperature

- Half cup white dry wine

- Two shallots, chopped.

- One tsp fresh parsley perfectly chopped.

- Fish

- Two tbsps. olive oil (extra virgin)

- One tsp salt

- Two (8 ounces) fish white fillets

- Half tsp ground black pepper

## Instructions

1. Combine white wine, garlic, and shallots in a small size pot.

2. Cook on high heat till the liquid has been lowered by half. Then remove it from the heat & allow it to cool slightly. Once the combination is warm, add the butter and stir all together. Season with parsley, pepper, and salt.

3. Refrigerate for a minimum of thirty minutes after covering with the plastic wrap. Enable to come to a room temp before grilling. Heat the grill to high heat.

4. Drizzle olive oil over the fillets & season with pepper and salt. Grill the fish for four minutes on each side, or till golden brown and easily flaked with a fork.

5. Put the fish on plates & drizzle with butter sauce. Serve instantly over hot pasta or, if you desire, with shrimp as a substitute for seafood.

# Pork chops (Tex-mex)

Preparation time: 17mins

Servings: 4

## Ingredients

- Four pork loin chops along with bone (around 1 1/2 lb/750 g total)
- Two tsps chili powder
- One tsp salt
- One tbsp brown sugar
- Two tsps ground cumin
- One tbsp vegetable oil

## Instructions

1. Combine the cumin, chili powder, brown sugar, and salt in a small mixing bowl. Mix in the oil thoroughly. The pork chops should be rubbed with the combination. (You can also do this phase ahead of time and store them in the refrigerator till the next day.)

2. Preheat the grill to medium. Brush the grill with a thin coating of oil. Preheat the grill for the pork chops. Close the BBQ grill's cover. Cook for five to seven minutes, or till the pork is slightly pink inside. (Pork chops should be turned in the mid of cooking).

# World's greatest-grilled steak

Preparation time: 5mins

Servings: 4

## Ingredients

- Two tsps. olive oil
- Two tsps. ketchup
- Four-five beef steaks
- One tsp oregano
- One tsp pepper
- Half cup low-level sodium soy sauce
- One tsp minced garlic

## Instructions

1. Mix all ingredients in a blender and pour it over the steaks.

2. Marinate for a minimum of 3 hours, turning occasionally.

3. Grill to your preference.

# Grilled garlic lime chicken with a mango salsa

Preparation time: 30mins

Servings: 4

## Ingredients

- Four garlic cloves
- Four boneless & skinless chicken breasts
- One large lime
- One tbsp olive oil

## Mango salsa

- One sweet red pepper or one sweet yellow pepper chopped & seeded
- One serrano pepper
- Two ripened mangoes peeled and minced.
- Three ripened Roma tomatoes, minced.
- Two green onions, minced
- Four cups short-grain steamed cooked (brown) rice
- One-two tbsp sugar (if mangoes are not extremely sweet)
- 1/4 cup, minced fresh cilantro
- One lime, juiced
- pepper & salt

## Instructions

1. In the bag (zip lock), marinate chicken with the oil's juice, one lime & the garlic for a minimum of 2 hours or all night.

2. To make the salsa, add all the ingredients in a mixing bowl and season to taste with pepper and salt. Set it aside to allow the flavors to combine. In the Meantime, grill chicken breasts at low heat until no longer pink.

3. To serve, put one cup of rice on every plate, top with chicken breast & divide salsa among the four plates.

4. Time does not contain the time of marinating or steaming rice.

# T-bone grilled steaks

Preparation time: 20mins

Servings: 2

## Ingredients

- Two tbsps. brown sugar
- Two tbsps. lemon juice
- Half cup of water
- Half cup soy sauce (light)
- Two tbsps. red wine vinegar
- Half tsp garlic powder
- Two tbsps. olive oil (extra virgin)
- One tbsp McCormick's Montreal Brand (steak seasoning)
- Two-three garlic cloves crashed.
- Two beef T-bone steaks (one in thick)
- Half tsp chipotle hot sauce
- 1/4 tsp, pepper

## Instructions

1. Mix the first eleven ingredients in a big resealable bag (plastic).

2. Add in the steaks.

3. Close the bag and coat it.

4. Refrigerate for the whole night, turning as needed.

5. Drain & discard marinade.

6. Grill the steaks for around five minutes on each side on high heat or desired consistency. (For the medium-rare, the meat thermometer must read one hundred and forty-five degrees, medium, one hundred and sixty degrees, well-done one hundred and seventy degrees).

# Grilled marinated tuna steak

Preparation time: 8hrs 10mins

Servings: 4

## Ingredients

- lemon pepper (just for taste) or ground black pepper (just for taste)
- Three (four ounces) tuna steaks, fresh

## Marinade

- One tbsp hoisin sauce
- Two tbsps. minced fresh parsley
- One tbsp lemon juice/one tbsp lime juice
- 1/4 cup, orange juice
- 1/4 cup, soy sauce
- Three tbsps. oil
- Three garlic cloves, chopped(optional)

## Instructions

1. In a mixing bowl, whisk together all the marinade ingredients until smooth.

2. In the shallow glass bowl, put the tuna steaks.

3. Put the marinade on tuna steaks & turn it to coat.

4. Cover in plastic wrap.

5. Refrigerate for eight to twenty-four hours.

6. Preheat the grill to a high setting.

7. Spray grill grate with oil.

8. Take off the steaks from the marinade and put them on a plate, discarding any remaining marinade.

9. Season both sides gently with fresh ground black pepper.

10. Grill steaks for five minutes on each side on the grill, or till rare or a medium-rare (not overcook tuna; otherwise, it would be dry.).

# Coffee-soaked steak

Preparation time: 20mins

Servings: 2-4

## Ingredients

- One tsp cayenne pepper
- Good quality pinch salt
- Three sweet potatoes, peeled & cut into chips/wedges
- One tbsp coffee, ground
- One tbsp paprika
- Six tbsps. olive oil
- One bone (in rib) eye steak, 1 ½ inch thick
- Two freshly thyme sprigs
- One pinch pepper
- One garlic clove
- Two tbsps. butter
- Two cups Brussels sprouts cut down.

## Instructions

1. Preheat the oven to a minimum of 390 degrees Fahrenheit.

2. Distribute Brussel sprouts on a baking tray, do the same for sweet potatoes. Sprinkle each with a two Tablespoon of olive oil & season with pepper and salt. Roast for a minimum of fifteen to twenty-five minutes or till golden (you can shake or flip on every seven mins to get color).

3. Twenty minutes earlier to cooking, take the steak out of the refrigerator & wrap all over with a coffee rub. Season each side with the salt & let it come to room temperature.

4. Put two Tbsp oil to a searing warm pan (if possible, cast iron) & put your steak; it would be genuinely winning sizzle. Cook the steak on all the sides for 45 secs, add in garlic, thyme, and butter, then flip every fifteen seconds for additional three-four minutes drizzling the butter on the steak.

5. Put in the oven, or switch to roasting tray & cook for a minimum of five minutes if the pan is oven safe (Every steak is changed, but for the medium-rare, you desire it to be soft then spring back when touched in the center).

6. Take it off from the oven & set it aside for at least 6-8 minutes to cool before slicing.

7. Serve it with your preferred sides, i.e., sweet potato fries & balsamic vinegar (roasted).

# Simply tasty grilled salmon

preparation time: 27mins

Servings: 2

## Ingredients

- Two tbsps. butter
- Onion, (to taste)
- Garlic, (taste)
- One lb. freshly salmon
- Salt, (taste)

## Instructions

1. Preheat your grill.

2. Put the salmon on a tinfoil sheet (adequate foil to fully wrap fillet). Melt the butter and drizzle it on salmon (on the other hand, you can only cut it up, however melting it would help it soak the fish). To taste, season with garlic, onion, and salt.

3. Cover the salmon in foil and seal it.

4. Grill it for around 15 minutes (or until over, depending on how warm the grill is), rotating every seven minutes.

# Steak with butter blue cheese

Preparation time: 35mins

Servings: 2

## Ingredients

- One tbsp minced fresh basil/ one tsp dried basil
- Half cup butter or half cup margarine softened
- One tbsp minced parsley
- One clove garlic, chopped
- Two beef T-bone steaks/ two porterhouse steaks
- Half cup crumbled blue cheese

## Instructions

1. Add butter, basil, blue cheese, parsley, and garlic in a small mixing bowl.

2. Place aside.

3. Grill the steaks to ideal doneness on the grill.

4. Drizzle a generous amount of the butter mixture over each steak.

5. Set aside the remaining butter to be used later.

6. (Try butter mixture with warm cooked vegetables).

# Grilled pizza

Preparation time: 30mins

Servings: 12

## Ingredients

- 1 (1 lb.) package frozen bread dough

Toppings of your choice

- fresh asparagus
- onion
- shaved parmesan cheese
- prosciutto
- sliced tomatoes
- herbs (etc.)

## For the seasoning

- 1 cup extra virgin olive oil
- 2 tsps. Ground oregano
- 1 tsp onion powder
- 3⁄4 tsp ground black pepper
- 1⁄2 tsp curry powder
- 1⁄2 tsp salt
- 1⁄2 tsp garlic powder
- 1⁄2 tsp red pepper flakes
- 1⁄4 tsp ground cumin
- 1⁄4 tsp cayenne pepper
- Chopped tomato (optional)
- Chopped onion (optional)
- Chopped fresh basil (optional)

## Instructions

1. For the seasoning, mix all seasoning ingredients in a small size saucepan. Stir on low heat till warm & oil becomes fragranced. Take off from heat & allow rest for a minimum of two hours at ordinary room temperature.

2. For Pizza bread: Delicately flour back of 15 x 10 inches of baking sheet & one of the dough pizza balls. Stretch the dough to the size of a baking sheet. Put the extended dough on the back of a baking sheet.

3. Combine the seasoned oil & generously brush the dough's surface. Flip the baking sheet and dough straight onto the cooking grate (similar to a large spatula). Take off the baking sheet from the oven and generously brush the dough with seasoned oil.

4. Grill for a minimum of 1 to 3 minutes over direct medium heat until the dough's underside is well marked. If crust bubbles, do not worry; it will be disappeared when you turned over.

5. Put the dough on the baking sheet & grill the side that has not been grilled. Keep on grilling for three to four minutes after brushing the top with additional oil.

6. Take off from the grill and place on the cooling rack to cool slightly. Go Back to the grill, close the cover, and cook to the required doneness (i.e., cheese melts, etc.) Repeat the grilling process with the remaining two dough balls.

# Turkey grilled burgers with poblano pickle relish & Monterey jack,

Preparation time: 30mins

Servings: 4

## Ingredients

### Poblano relish

- One poblano chile, grilled, stripped, seeded, & finely cut
- Two standard dill pickle, finely cut
- One little red onion, finely sliced
- 1/4 cup fresh lime juice
- 1 tsp honey
- 2 tbsps. finely chopped fresh cilantro leaves
- 1/4 tsp fresh ground black pepper

### Avocado mayonnaise

- 1/4 tsp, kosher salt
- 1/4 tsp, freshly ground black pepper
- One tbsp lime juice
- Half tsp ground cumin
- Half ripened Hass avocado, peeled & chopped
- 1/4 cup, mayonnaise
- Two garlic cloves, minced

### Turkey burgers

- 1 1/2 lbs. ground turkey (99% lean)
- Two tbsps. canola oil
- Half tsp kosher salt
- Half tsp fresh ground black pepper
- Four slices (Half oz each) Monterey jack cheese

## Instructions

1. Poblano Pickle Relish: In a medium mixing bowl, put all the relish ingredients. Until serving, cover and set aside for a minimum of thirty minutes & up to four hours at room temperature.

2. Avocado Mayonnaise: In a food processor, combine all the mayonnaise ingredients & process till smooth.

3. Turkey Burgers: Preheat the grill to high heat. Form the ground turkey into four round patties around1 1/2-inch thick with hands. Brush each side of the burger with oil & season with pepper and salt. Grill for a minimum of 4 minutes on each side, or till lightly charred on both sides & cooked through. Put a slice of the cheese on every burger, covered the grill lid, & cook for an additional minute to allow the cheese to melt. Place on a plate and set aside for at least 5 minutes to cool.

4. Spread 1 tbsp avocado mayonnaise & a few tbsps. relish on each burger. If needed, serve the residual avocado mayonnaise on the side.

5. Bobby Flay grills chiles and peppers directly on the grill. Boost the temperature of the grill to high. Season peppers with salt & pepper after brushing with the olive oil. Grill for eight to ten minutes, or till charred on each side. Fill a bowl halfway with peppers, cover it with the plastic wrap & set aside for fifteen minutes. Peel, stem, halve and seed them after that. Crusted on the grill.

# Crusted grilled steak with lemon butter.

Preparation time: 50mins

Servings: 4

## Ingredients

## Lemon butter

- One tbsp lemon juice
- 1/4 tsp, garlic powder
- Four tbsps. butter (softened)
- One tbsp minced fresh parsley

## Steak

- One tbsp, salt
- One tsp garlic powder
- Four sirloin steaks
- 1/4 cup, ground black pepper Half tsp red pepper flakes
- One tsp ground coriander
- 1 1/2 tsps., white pepper
- 1/4 cup, sugar

## Instructions

1. Combine the parsley, lemon juice, butter, and 1/4 tsp garlic powder in a mixing bowl.

2. Put the butter mixture into a log shape using plastic wrap.

3. Refrigerate till firm.

4. Add the red pepper flakes, black pepper, white pepper, coriander, garlic powder, sugar, and salt, in a large mixing bowl.

5. Rub the spice mixture all over the steaks on each side.

6. Shake off the leftover.

7. Put the steaks for two minutes on a warm grill.

8. Flip & cook for another 2 minutes.

9. Move the steak to the slight chiller part of the grill & cook till required doneness.

10. Drizzle a slice of lemon butter over each steak.

# Grilled shrimp

Preparation time: 16mins

Servings: 4

## Ingredients

## For the rub

- one tbsp garlic salt
- Half tbsp black pepper
- one tbsp paprika
- one tbsp garlic powder
- one tbsp Italian seasoning

## For the shrimp

- Two lbs. medium-size shrimp, peeled & deveined
- Two tbsps. olive oil

## Instructions

1. Place olive oil and shrimp in a one-gallon plastic food container, flip to coat, drizzle sufficient rub to cover the shrimp.
2. The bag must be dark red.
3. Chill for up to four hours; the longer you leave, the more chiller they will get.
4. Preheat the grill and skewer the shrimp as it heats up.
5. When the coals are hot, clean the shrimp's surface and rub it with a rag dipped in canola oil (use a glove, please).
6. Put shrimp on an oiled grill and cook for 2 to 3 mins, then rotate and cook for another 2-3 mins.
7. Remove the skewers and present them immediately.
8. There is no need for a dipping sauce.

# Porterhouse grilled steak with parmesan-paprika butter

Preparation time: 2hrs 35mins

Servings: 4

## Ingredients

- 1 (2 3/4 lb.) porterhouse steaks, 2-3/4 to 3 inch thick
- 1/4 cup olive oil
- Seven large garlic cloves, minced
- One tbsp fresh thyme, chopped
- One tbsp salt
- 2 tsps. ground black pepper
- One tsp fresh rosemary, chopped

## Paprika-parmesan butter

- 1/4 tsp, hot pepper sauce
- One tsp paprika
- Three tbsps. butter, room temperature
- Two tsps. grated parmesan cheese
- Half tsp Dijon mustard
- Half tsp Worcestershire sauce
- 1/4 tsp, ground black pepper

## Instructions

1. In a small mixing bowl, combine all the ingredients for the Parmesan-Paprika Butter. (This dish can be prepared up to two days ahead of time.) Apply at ordinary room temperature.

2. Arrange the steak in a baking dish made of glass.

3. In a small mixing bowl, whisk together the oil and succeeding five ingredients. Half of the marinade should be poured over the steak. Turn the steak over and brush with the remaining marinade. Cover and relax for more than 2 hrs. or approximately 24 hrs., turning now and then.

4. Preheat the grill (moderate heat).

5. Shake off any leftover marinade from the steak.

6. Put the steak on the grill and cover it.

7. Grill the steak to desired consistency (around 15 mins on each side, or 125 degrees Fahrenheit to 130 degrees Fahrenheit for moderate-rare, approximately 18 mins on each side), sometimes transferring steak to a slightly cool portion of the rack when cooking too rapidly.

8. Arrange the steak on a platter and wrap it to keep it warm. Enable for a 5-minute rest time.

9. Cut the meat apart from the bone with a sharp knife. Each meat portion should be cut into thick slices (1/3 inch).

10. To serve, spread Parmesan-Paprika Butter on top of the slices. This rub is also perfect over chicken wings.

# Grilled Brussels Sprouts

Preparation time: 30 mins

Servings: 4

## Ingredients

- Sixteen Brussels sprouts (at least 1/2" diameter), fresh & trimmed.

- One medium sweet red pepper.

- One medium onion.

- Half tsp salt.

- Half tsp garlic powder.

- 1/4 tsp coarsely pepper (ground).

- One tbsp olive oil.

## Instructions

1. Put the steamer basket across One inch of water in a big saucepan. Carry a kettle of water to a rolling boil. In a basket, position the Brussels sprouts. Reduce heat to sustain a boil, then steam for 4-6 mins, sealed, until crisp-tender. Allow to cool slowly before cutting every sprout in half.

2. Peel & cut the red pepper n onion into 1-1/2-inch sections. Thread red pepper, Brussels sprouts, & onion alternately on four metal / soaked wooden skewers. Combine the garlic powder, salt, & pepper in a bowl. Brush the vegetables with oil & season with salt n pepper. Grill over medium heat, covered, or broil 4 inches away from the heat until the vegetables are soft, 10-12 mins.

# Grilled Chicken Burgers

Preparation time: 30 mins

servings: 4

## Ingredients

- one medium tart apple (peeled & finely chopped)
- one small onion (finely chopped)
- one celery rib (finely chopped)
- salt, 1/4 tsp
- 1/4 tsp poultry seasoning
- Dash pepper
- one lb. chicken (ground)
- 1/4 cup cranberry sauce (whole berry)
- one tbsp mayonnaise
- four hamburger buns (split)
- (optional) Bibb lettuce leaves

## Instructions

1. Add the first 6 ingredients in a big mixing bowl. Mix well after crumbling the chicken over the mixture. Make four patties out of the mixture.

2. Cook for 10-12 mins on an indoor grill or till the thermometer reads 165° F.

3. Add the cranberry sauce & mayonnaise in a shallow mixing cup. Serve the burgers on the buns with some cranberry sauce & salad, if needed.

# Bruschetta Steak

Preparation time: 25 mins

servings: 4

## Ingredients

- Three medium tomatoes (chopped)

- Three tbsp basil

- Three tbsp parsley

- Two tbsp olive oil

- One tsp oregano (fresh & minced) / half tsp oregano (dried)

- One garlic clove (minced)

- 3/4 tsp salt (divided)

- One beef iron (flat) / one lb. top sirloin steak, cut in four portions

- 1/4 tsp pepper

- Optional - Parmesan cheese (Grated)

## Instructions

1. Combine the first six ingredients; stir in 1/4 teaspoon salt.

2. Sprinkle beef with pepper & remaining salt. Grill, covered, over medium heat or broil 4 in. from heat until meat reaches desired doneness (for medium-rare, a thermometer should read 135° F; medium, 140° F), 4-6 mins per side. Top it with tomato mixture. If desired, sprinkle with cheese.

# Lime and Sesame Grilled Eggplant

Preparation time: 20 mins

servings: 4

## Ingredients

- 3 tbsp lime juice
- One tbsp sesame oil
- Half tsp sodium soy sauce (reduced)
- Onne garlic clove (minced)
- Half tsp ginger root (grated & fresh) / 1/4 tsp ginger (ground)
- Half tsp salt
- 1/8 tsp pepper
- One medium 1/4 lb. eggplant, cut in half-inch slices (lengthwise)
- Two tsp honey
- 1/8 tsp red pepper flakes (crushed)
- Green onion & sesame seeds (Thinly sliced)

## Instructions

1. Whisk the first seven ingredients together in a small bowl until smooth; brush two tbsp of the juice mixture on both sides of the eggplant slices. Cover & grill till it gets soft, around 4-6 mins per hand, over medium heat.

2. Arrange eggplant on a plate to serve. Drizzle leftover juice mixture over eggplant with honey & pepper flakes. Green onion & sesame seeds are sprinkled on top.

# Spicy Lemon Chicken Kabobs

Preparation time: 25 mins

servings: 6

## Ingredients

- 1/4 cup, juice of lemon
- Four tbsps. olive oil (split)
- Three tbsps. white wine
- Half tsp pepper flakes (red & crushed)
- One tsp rosemary (minced & fresh) / 1/4 tsp rosemary (dried & crushed)
- Half lb. chicken boneless breasts (skinless), cut in cubes (1-inch)
- Two lemons (halved)
- Chopped chives

## Instructions

1. Add lemon juice, wine, 3 tbsp oil, pepper flakes, & rosemary in a big shallow bowl. Toss in the chicken & toss to cover. Refrigerate for up to three hrs.

2. Rinse the chicken & toss out the marinade. 6 soaked / metal wooden skewers threaded with chicken. Grill for about 10-12 mins, sealed, over moderate heat till no lengthier pink, turning one time.

3. In the meantime, put the lemons cut side down on the grill. Grill for 8-10 mins, or till it gets lightly browned. Lemon halves can be squeezed over the chicken. Drizzle it with the remaining oil and chives.

# Zesty Grilled Ham

Preparation time: 15 mins

servings: 4

## Ingredients

- 1/3 cup brown sugar (packed)
- Two tbsps. prepared horseradish
- Four tsp lemon juice
- One bone-in ham 1 lb. steak (fully cooked)

## Instructions

1. In a shallow saucepan, combine the horseradish, brown sugar, & lemon juice; Boil it, stirring continuously. Brush both sides of the ham.

2. Barbecue the ham on a grill rack that has been oiled over medium heat. Grill, sealed, for 7-10 mins, or till glazed & cooked through, rotating periodically.

# Ultimate Grilled Pork Chops

Preparation time: 30 mins

servings: 4

## Ingredients

- 1/4 cup, kosher salt
- 1/4 cup, sugar
- Two cups of water
- Two cups of ice water
- Four pork rib (center-cut chops) about 1" thick & 8 ounces
- Two tbsps. canola oil
- Basic rub
- Three tbsps. paprika
- One tsp of onion powder, garlic powder, ground mustard & ground cumin
- One tsp coarsely pepper (ground)
- Half tsp chipotle pepper (ground)

## Instructions

1. Mix salt, sugar, & two cups of water in a big saucepan; boil & stir it over medium heat till the salt & sugar gets dissolved. Remove the pan from the sun. To get the brine to room temp, add two cups of ice water.

2. Mix pork chops & cooled brine in a big resealable plastic container. Switch it to coat chops & seal bag, squeezing out enough air as possible. Fill a 13x9-inch baking dish with the mixture. Refrigerate for 8-12 hrs.

3. Remove the chops from the brine, drain them, and pat them dry. Remove the brine and discard it. Using a brush, coat all sides of the chops in grease. Combine rub ingredients in a small bowl & rub them over the pork chops. Allow 30 mins to come to room temp.

4. Cover & grill chops for 4-6 mins on either side over medium heat on an oiled rack, or till the thermometer measures 145° F. Allow for five min of resting time before serving.

# Scrum-Delicious Burger

Preparation time: 30 mins

servings: 6

## Ingredients

- Half lb. beef (ground)
- Three tbsps. Onion (finely chopped)
- Half tsp garlic salt
- Half tsp pepper
- One cup cheddar cheese (shredded)
- 1/3 cup, mushrooms (canned sliced)
- Six bacon strips (crumbled & cooked)
- 1/4 cup, mayonnaise
- Six hamburger buns (split)
- optional - Lettuce leaves & tomato slices

## Instructions

1. Combine the onion, beef, garlic salt, & pepper in the big mixing bowl. Make 6 patties that are 3/4 inch thick.

2. Combine the onions, cheese, bacon, & mayonnaise in a little bowl & chill.

3. Cover & grill burgers over medium heat for about 5-7 mins on either side or till the thermometer reads 160°F. Spoon some cheese mixture(1/4cup) on every burger in the last Three mins of cooking. If wanted, serve on buns with lettuce and tomato.

# Grilled Garlic Naan

Preparation time: 10 mins

servings: 4

## Ingredients

- Two tbsps. butter (melted)
- Three garlic cloves (minced)
- Two naan flatbreads

## Instructions

1. Combine the garlic & butter. Place the naan on the grill rack & cook for two mins over medium-high heat or till the bottom is golden brown. Brush the end of garlic butter before flipping. Grill until the bottom is golden orange.

# Chapter 3: Smokeless Grill Recipes

## Pan-Grilled Salmon with Red Pepper Salsa

Preparation time: 16 mins

Servings: 4

**Ingredients**

**Salmon:**

- Two tsp chili powder
- One tsp ground cumin
- Half tsp salt.
- Half tsp ground coriander
- One-Quarter tsp chipotle chile powder (ground)
- Four (Six-ounce) salmon fillets (skinless)
- Cooking spray

**Salsa:**

- One cup prechopped red bell pepper
- One-Quarter cup chopped tomato.

- Two tsps. prechopped red onion
- 1 tsp chopped fresh cilantro.
- One Half tsp fresh lime juice
- ⅛ tsp salt

**Instructions**

1. Preheat a grill skillet over medium heat for the salmon. Rub the first five ingredients equally over the fillets. Oil the plate with cooking spray. Cook for 4 mins on either side or until an optimal degree of doneness is reached.

2. When the fish is frying, make the salsa. In a mixing cup, mix the bell pepper and the rest of the ingredients. Eat salsa with the fillets.

# Pan-Grilled Thai Tuna Salad

Preparation time: 15 mins

Servings: 2

## Ingredients

- Cooking spray
- Two (6-ounce) tuna steaks of Yellowfin
- One Quarter tsp salt
- ⅛ tsp black pepper
- Four cups napa cabbage (lightly sliced)
- One cup cucumber (lightly sliced)
- Half cup matchstick-cut carrots
- ⅓ cup red onion (pre-sliced)
- One (chopped) navel orange, (sectioned)
- One tsp sugar
- Two tsp fresh cilantro (chopped)
- Two tsp lime juice, fresh
- Two tsp rice vinegar
- Half tsp dark sesame oil

- One-Quarter tsp oelek Sriracha sambal (hot chile sauce) or (ground fresh chile paste)

**Instructions**

1. Preheat a grill pan to medium-high. Oil the plate with cooking spray. Season the fish with pepper and salt to taste. Cook for two mins on either side or until the target degree of doneness is reached. Place on a cutting board to cool.

2. Combine cabbage with the following four ingredients in a large mixing cup. Merge the sugar and the remaining ingredients in a small cup. Set aside one tablespoon of dressing. Toss the salad with the remaining dressing and toss gently to blend. Equally, divide the salad combination into two bowls. Place every tuna steak over the salad mixture, cut into 1/4-inch slices around the grain. 1 1/2 teaspoon dressing, set aside, sprinkled over every serving.

3. To serve, place two cups coconut sorbet in each of two dessert bowls, cover with two tbsps diced skinned mango, & one tbsp toasted coconut (flaked & sweetened).

# Grilled Chicken with Mustard-Tarragon Sauce

Preparation time: 25 mins

Servings: 4

## Ingredients

- Four (6-ounce) chicken breast halves (boneless), skinless
- Half tsp salt, (divided)
- One-Quarter tsp black pepper, (divided)
- Cooking spray
- Three tsp shallots (minced)
- Three tsp Dijon mustard
- Two tsp red wine (vinegar)
- Two tsp water
- One tsp olive oil, extra-virgin
- One tsp fresh tarragon (chopped)
- Half tsp sugar

- Four cups gourmet greens salad

**Instructions**

1. Preheat a barbeque grill over high heat. 1/8 tbsp pepper and 1/4 tbsp salt are evenly distributed over the chicken. Using nonstick cooking oil, coat the pan. Cook the meat in the pan for 6 mins on either side or until cooked through.

2. In a mixing cup, whisk together the existing 1/4 teaspoon salt, the remaining 1/8 teaspoon pepper, the shallots, and the following six components. Serve the chicken with the sauce over the greens.

# Catfish Sandwiches with Creole Mayonnaise

Preparation time: 30 mins

Servings: 4

## Ingredients

- Cooking spray
- Four catfish fillets (6-ounce)
- One Half tsp Cajun (seasoning)
- Four hamburger buns (1 1/2-ounce)
- Three tsp mayonnaise, fat-free
- One Half tsp shallots (minced)
- One Quarter tsp Dijon mustard (whole grain)
- Half tsp lemon juice, fresh
- Four curly leaf lettuce leaves
- Four slices tomato (1/4-inch-thick)
- Eight tsp sweet pickle relish

## Instructions

1. Preheat a grill pan to medium-high. Oil the plate with nonstick cooking spray. Season the fillets uniformly with salt and pepper. Cook for 4 mins after adding the fillets to the

plate. Cook for 3 minutes on the other hand, or till fish flakes easily when checked with a fork, or until an optimal degree of doneness is achieved.

2. Put buns, slice sides down in the pan, and toast for one minute. Remove the pan from the heat.

3. Whisk together the mustard, shallots, mayonnaise, and milk. One lettuce leaf should be put on the bottom half of each bun; one fillet and one tomato slice should be placed on top of each serving. Cover each tomato with two teaspoons relish. Place a tsp of the mayonnaise mixture on the cut side of each top Half of buns, top with each sandwich.

# Butcher's Cut Sliders

Preparation time: 58 mins

Servings: 4

## Ingredients

- Five tsps. red wine vinegar (divided)
- One tsp sugar
- Half cup lightly sliced shallots
- Half ounce sirloin (ground)
- One Quarter tsp salt
- One-Quarter tsp black pepper (freshly ground)
- Cooking spray
- One tsp olive oil, extra-virgin
- One tsp Dijon mustard
- One tsp soy sauce, lower sodium
- One or Half cups arugula
- One tsp fresh chives
- Two tbsp canola mayonnaise
- One ounce (crumbled) blue cheese (1/4 cup)
- Eight sourdough slider buns

## Instructions

1. In a tiny bowl, mix 1/4 cup sugar and vinegar before sugar dissolves. Toss the shallots in the vinegar mixture. Refrigerate for 30 mins after covering. Toss it in the air. Drain the water and put it aside.

2. Separate meat into eight equal pieces; carefully shape each piece into a 1/4-inch-thick patty, being careful not to overwork the meat. Season all sides of the patties with pepper and salt. Preheat a grill pan to medium-high. Oil the plate with nonstick cooking spray. Cook 2 mins on either side or until the target degree of doneness is reached; do not push on patties while cooking.

3. In a big mixing cup, whisk together the remaining one teaspoon mustard, oil, soy sauce, vinegar. Toss in the arugula and chives gently to coat. In a shallow mixing dish, combine mayonnaise and cheese. Spread around 2 tsp mayonnaise mixture on the lower half of

each bun. 1/4 cup arugula mixture, one patty, 1 tsp pickled shallot, and one bun top on each slider.

# Grass-Fed Beef Tenderloin Steaks with Sautéed Mushrooms

Preparation time: 45 mins

Servings: 4 servings

**Ingredients**

- One tsp olive oil, extra-virgin
- Four shallots (peeled and quartered)
- Two tsp fresh thyme (chopped)
- ⅛ tsp salt
- ⅛ tsp red pepper (crushed)
- Three (4-ounce) mushroom blend packages (pre-sliced) exotic
- Two garlic cloves (minced)
- One-Quarter cup dry sherry or Madeira wine
- One tsp soy sauce, low sodium
- Two tsp fresh parsley (chopped)
- Cooking spray
- Four (4-ounce) grass-fed beef tenderloin steaks, trimmed (one inch thick)
- Half tsp salt.
- One-Quarter tsp black pepper (freshly ground)

**Instructions**

1. In a broad nonstick skillet, heat the oil over medium-high heat. Sauté for 3 mins, or until shallots are finely browned. Sauté for 6 mins, or until lightly browned, with thyme, 1/8 tbsp cinnamon, smashed red pepper, and mushrooms. Sauté for 2 minutes after adding the garlic. Stir in the wine, then soy sauce, and simmer for 15 seconds, or until the liquid has almost entirely evaporated. Wrap and set aside after adding the parsley.

2. Preheat a grill pan to medium-high. Oil the plate with nonstick cooking spray. Season the steaks with half a teaspoon of pepper and salt. Add the steaks to the pan and cook for 3 mins on either side or until cooked to your liking. Allow for a 5-mine rest period, with the mushroom mixture to the other.

3. Wine pairing: Offer vegetation beef with a full-bodied, mild red to round out the leanness. Many varietals will fit, but cabernet sauvignon has a particular beef preference due to its structure and depth.

# Hoisin Grilled Sirloin

Preparation time: 18 mins

Servings: 4

## Ingredients

- Two tsp hoisin sauce
- One tsp apricot (preserves)
- One Half tsp lime juice (fresh)
- ⅛ tsp red pepper (crushed)
- Salt Half tsp
- One-pound top sirloin

## Instructions

1. Heat a grill pan over medium-high heat.

2. Blend the components in a mixing dish. First four components. Season the beef with salt. Apply the beef to the pan and cook for 3 mins on either side or till cooked to your taste. Allow for a 5-mins rest before slicing. Brush the hoisin paste on all sides of the meat. Thinly slice the beef through the grain.

# Chipotle Taco Salad (Rubbed & Shrimp)

Preparation time: 20 mins

Servings: 4

## Ingredients

- Three tsp fresh cilantro (chopped)
- Three tsp minced shallots
- Three tsp lime juice, fresh
- Two tsp honey
- ⅛ tsp salt
- Two tbsp olive oil
- One frozen (eight-inch) flour tortilla salad-shell (such as Azteca)
- One-pound deveined giant shrimp (peeled)
- Half tsp chili powder
- One-Quarter tsp chile powder of chipotle (ground)
- ⅛ tsp salt
- Spray (Cooking)
- Six cups romaine hearts prechopped packaged
- One-Half cups sliced skinned ripe mango (1 large)
- Half cup cherry tomatoes
- Four radishes (quartered)

## Instructions

1. 350 degrees Fahrenheit Preheat the oven (180 degrees Celsius).

2. In a shallow mixing cup, whisk together the first five ingredients. Gradually drizzle in the grease, whisking continuously.

3. Toasted tortilla shells should be baked at 350°F according to the box instructions.

4. Preheat a grill skillet over medium heat as the shells roast. In a big mixing cup, combine the shrimp, chili powders, and salt; toss well to cover. Oil the plate with nonstick cooking spray. Heat for 2 mins on each end or till shrimp is thoroughly cooked.

5. Combine the spinach, pineapple, onion, and radishes in a salad bowl. Toss the salad in the vinaigrette to cover it. In each tortilla shell, place around 1 1/2 cup salad; split shrimp equally among salads.

# Grilled Chicken Breasts with Plum Salsa

Preparation time: 20 mins

Servings: 4

## Ingredients

- Chicken:
- Two tbsp brown sugar
- Salt Half tbsp
- Half tbsp cumin (ground)
- One Quarter tsp garlic powder
- Four (4-ounce) skinless chicken breast halves (boneless)
- Two tbsp vegetable oil
- Plum Salsa:
- One cup ripe plum, chopped (2 plums)
- Two tbsp or One tsp fresh, dried cilantro (chopped)
- Two tsp red onion (chopped)
- Two tsp cider vinegar
- One-Quarter tsp hot sauce
- ⅛ tsp salt

## Instructions

1. To make the chicken, add the first four ingredients to a mixing bowl. Brown sugar mixture can be rubbed all over the chicken.

2. In a barbecue pan or nonstick skillet, heat the oil over medium heat. Cook for 6 mins on either side or until chicken is cooked.

3. In a mixing dish, combine the remaining ingredients while the chicken is frying. Serve alongside chicken.

# Beef Lettuce Wraps

Preparation time: 30 mins

Servings: 4

## Ingredients

- Cooking spray
- One (1-pound) flank steak (trimmed)
- One-Quarter tsp kosher salt
- One-Quarter tsp black pepper (freshly ground)
- Three tsp lime juice, fresh
- Two tsp fish sauce
- Four tsp dark brown sugar
- One jalapeño pepper (seeded and minced)
- Eight Bibb lettuce leaves
- One cup red onion (lightly sliced)
- One cup is torn mint (fresh)
- Half cup matchstick-cut English cucumber
- A half-cup is torn cilantro (fresh)
- Two tsp unsalted dry-roasted peanuts (chopped)

## Instructions

1. Preheat a grill pan to medium-high. Oil the plate with nonstick cooking spray. Spice the steak with salt and pepper before serving. Place the steak in the pan and cook for 5 mins on either side or until target doneness is reached. Take Off from the pan and set aside for 10 mins. Thinly slice the beef horizontally around the grain.

2. In a medium mixing cup, whisk together the juice, jalapeno, sugar, and fish sauce in a shallow serving cup, set aside four teaspoons of the juice mixture. In a big mixing cup, pour the remaining juice mixture, apply the steak and toss to cover. In the middle of each lettuce leaf, place 1 1/2 ounces beef; top with two teaspoons onion, two teaspoons mint, one teaspoon cucumber, and one teaspoon cilantro. Roll up evenly sprinkled with peanuts. Serve with the juice combination that was set aside.

3. Soba noodle salad: Cook 6 ounces soba noodles, omitting salt and fat, according to box directions; rinse well. In a big mixing bowl, combine pasta, 1/3 cup sliced green onions, and 1/3 cup matchstick-cut carrots. In a tiny cup, whisk together 1 1/2 teaspoon rice vinegar, one teaspoon sesame oil, one teaspoon fish sauce, one teaspoon low-sodium soy sauce, two teaspoons sambal oelek, and one teaspoon brown sugar. Toss the noodle mixture with the vinegar mixture.

# Barbecued Pork Chops

Preparation time: 35 mins

Servings: 4

## Ingredients

- Two tsp sugar dark brown

- Two tsp soy sauce, low sodium

- One tsp dark sesame oil

- One tsp pineapple juice

- Two tsp fresh garlic (minced)

- One-Half tbsp's sake (rice wine)

- One-Quarter tsp red pepper (crushed)

- One-Quarter tsp black pepper (freshly ground)

- Four bone-in pork chops (1/2 inch thick)

- Cooking spray

- One-Quarter tsp kosher salt

- One tsp sesame seeds (toasted)

## Instructions

1. In a zip-top plastic container, mix the first eight ingredients; substitute the pork. Wrap and refrigerate at ambient temperature for 25 minutes.

2. Preheat a grill pan to medium-high. Oil the plate with nonstick cooking spray. Take the pork out of the bag and put it aside from the marinade. Season pork with salt and pepper. Pork should be cooked. Three minutes per hand for either side or until finished. Fill a shallow saucepan halfway with allocated marinade and bring to a simmer. Lower the temp and continue to cook for another 2 minutes, or until the sauce has thickened. Brush the pork with the decreased marinade and sesame seeds.

3. Kimchi-style slaw: In a big mixing bowl, whisk together 2 tsp minced garlic, 1 to 2 tsp Sriracha, 1/4 cup rice wine vinegar, 1 tsp minced fresh ginger, 1 tsp kosher salt, 1 tsp canola oil, and 1/2 tsp sugar. Toss in 4 cups Napa cabbage shredded and 1/2 cup thinly sliced green onions to cover.

# Pan-Grilled Snapper with Orzo Pasta Salad

Preparation time: 25 mins

Servings: 4

## Ingredients

- One Half cups orzo, uncooked
- Cooking spray
- 4 (6-ounce) red snapper fillets
- Half tsp salt (divided)
- One-Quarter tsp black pepper (divided)
- One Half tsp shallots (minced)
- One tsp fresh parsley (chopped)
- One tsp lemon juice, fresh
- Two tsp orange juice
- One tsp Dijon mustard
- Two Half tsp olive oil, extra-virgin

## Instructions

1. Add the noodles according to the package directions, ignoring the fat and salt. Drain and hold the water warm.

2. Preheat a grill pan to medium-high. Oil the plate with nonstick cooking spray. 1/4 teaspoon salt and 1/8 tbsp pepper are generously sprinkled over the fish. Cook 3 minutes on either hand, or till fish flakes easily when measured with a fork, or till optimal doneness is reached.

3. Combine the ingredients in a tiny cup and whisk to combine the remaining 1/4 tbsp salt, the remaining 1/8 tbsp pepper, the shallots, lemon juice, parsley, mustard orange juice. Steadily sprinkle in the olive oil when constantly whisking. Toss the spaghetti with the shallot mixture and toss well to coat.

# Chicken Souvlaki with Tzatziki Sauce

Preparation time: 50 mins

Servings: 2

## Ingredients

- Souvlaki:
- Three tsp lemon juice, fresh
- One Half or 1/2 tsp fresh, dried oregano (chopped)
- Two tsp olive oil
- Salt Half tsp
- Four garlic cloves (minced)
- Half pound skinless chicken breast (boneless) slice into (1-inch pieces)
- One zucchini (medium) quartered longwise and sliced into (1/2-inch-thick)
- Cooking spray
- Tzatziki Sauce:
- Half cup cucumber shredded, seeded, and (peeled)
- Half cup plain yogurt, low-fat
- One tsp lemon juice
- One Quarter tsp salt
- One garlic clove (minced)

## Instructions

1. In a zip-top plastic container, add the first five components for souvlaki; seal and mix to combine. Move the bag to hide the contents chicken. Refrigerate the chicken for 30 minutes, rotating once.

2. Remove the chicken from the container and toss out the marinade. Using 4 (8-inch) skewers, alternately thread the chicken and zucchini.

3. Set the temperature o fa grill pan to medium-high temperature with cooking spray. Cook, rotating once, for 8 mins or till chicken is cooked.

4. To make the tzatziki sauce, whisk together cucumber, cream, one teaspoon lemon juice, 1/4 tbsp salt, and one garlic clove. Tzatziki sauce goes along with souvlaki.

# Pineapple Chicken Satay

Preparation time: 20 mins

Servings: 4

## Ingredients

- One Quarter cup soy sauce, lower sodium
- One Quarter cup chili sauce sweet (just like Mae Ploy)
- One-Quarter cup crunchy peanut butter (natural style)
- Two tsp peanut oil
- Half tsp curry powder
- One pound chicken breast tenders slice longwise into (8 pieces)
- Cooking spray
- One Half cups pineapple (diced)
- ⅓ cup vertically red onion (sliced)
- Two tsp fresh cilantro (chopped)
- Two tsp lime juice, fresh
- ⅛ tsp red pepper (ground)

## Instructions

1. In a blending bowl, whisk together the first three components.

2. In a mixing dish, combine the peanut oil, curry powder, and chicken; shake to cover. 8 (6-inch) skewers threaded with chicken.

3. Preheat a grill pan to medium-high. Oil the plate with nonstick cooking spray. Bake for 4 minutes on either side or until chicken is cooked through.

4. Add2 tsp lime juice, 1/8 tsp ground red pepper, 2 tsp cilantro, 1 1/2 cups pineapple, and1/3 cup red onion in a mixing bowl as the chicken cooks. Serve the chicken with the pineapple and soy sauce combination.

# Grilled Grouper with Browned Butter-Orange Couscous

Preparation time: 30 mins

Servings: 4

## Ingredients

- Couscous:
- Two tsp butter
- One Quarter cup almonds (slivered)
- One cup couscous, uncooked
- One (14-ounce) chicken broth (fat-free) can (less-sodium)
- Half cup coarsely orange sections (chopped)
- One Quarter cup pomegranate seeds
- Three tsp fresh parsley (chopped)
- One Quarter tsp salt
- Grouper:
- One Quarter tsp salt
- Half tsp coriander seeds
- Half tsp black peppercorns
- Dash of red pepper (ground)
- 4 (6-ounce) fillets(ground)

- Cooking spray

**Instructions**

1. Melt the butter in a big stainless steel medium bowl to make couscous. Add the almonds and cook for 2 mins, or until the butter is finely browned and the almonds are toasted. Cook, stirring continuously, for 1 minute after introducing the couscous. Remove the pan from the grill.

2. In a medium skillet over high flame, bring broth to a simmer. Add broth in a slow, steady stream to the pan's couscous mixture; cover and set aside for 5 minutes. Using a fork, fluff the mixture. Combine the bananas, pomegranate seeds, parsley, and 1/4 teaspoon salt in a mixing dish.

3. To Cook grouper, red pepper, coriander, peppercorns, and finely ground 1/4 teaspoon salt r in a spice or coffee grinder. Rub the flavored cream all over the fish.

4. Preheat a grill pan to medium-high. Oil the plate with nonstick cooking spray. Put the fillets in the saucepan and cook for 4 mins. Cook for 4 mins, or till fish flakes easily when measured with a fork, or until an optimal doneness degree is reached. Serve alongside couscous.

5. Wine note: The key ingredients to remember are oranges in the couscous and dried coriander on the trout. It is proposed a Washington State Riesling. It's bright and bold, like the dish, with a delicate sweetness that rounds out the coriander's heaviness.

# Peach Spiced Lamb Chops

Preparation time: 15 mins

Servings: 4

## Ingredients

- One tsp brown sugar
- One tsp salt
- One tsp onion powder
- One tsp chili powder
- One tsp paprika
- Half tsp oregano, dried
- One Quarter tsp ginger (ground)
- One Quarter tsp allspice(ground)
- One-Quarter tsp black pepper
- 8 (4-ounce) bone-in lamb loin chops (trimmed)
- Cooking spray
- ⅓ cup peach preserves

## Instructions

1. In a small cup, mix the last nine components; rub the spice mixture equally on both sides of lamb chops.

2. Preheat a grill pan to medium-high. Oil the plate with nonstick cooking spray. Cook the lamb chops in the pan for 3 1/2 mins on either hand. 1 tsp preserves brushed on each chop Cook for 1 min on the other hand. Brush the remaining preserves across the chops. Remove the pan from the grill.

# Jamaican-Spiced Chicken Thighs

Preparation time: 15 mins

Servings: 4

## Ingredients

- One-Quarter cup red onion (minced)
- One tsp sugar
- One tsp finely seeded jalapeño pepper (chopped)
- Two tsp cider vinegar
- Two tsp soy sauce, low sodium
- Salt Half tsp
- Half tsp allspice (ground)
- Half tsp thyme, dried
- Half tsp black pepper
- One-Quarter tsp red pepper (ground)
- Eight chicken thighs boneless (1 1/2 pounds)
- Cooking spray

## Instructions

1. In a big mixing bowl, mix the first ten components; introduce the chicken and shake to cover. Preheat a grill pan to medium-high. Oil the plate with nonstick cooking spray. Cook for 4 mins after adding the chicken to the pan. Cook for another 6 mins or until chicken is cooked.

# Panini Margherita

Preparation time: 14 mins

Servings: 4

## Ingredients

- 16(Two large tomatoes) plum tomato slices (1/8-inch-thick)
- 8 (1-ounce) French bread loaf portions rustic
- One Quarter tsp salt
- One-Quarter tsp black pepper (freshly ground)
- 1 cup (4 ounces) mozzarella cheese (shredded)
- 12 fresh basil leaves
- 8 tsp olive oil, extra-virgin (divided)
- Cooking spray

## Instructions

1. Spread tomato slices thinly over four toast slices and season with salt and pepper to taste. Over the onions, thinly distribute the cheese. Distribute basil leaves equally over cheese, then top with the remaining 4 bits of toast. Cover each sandwich in cooking spray and drizzle 1 tsp olive oil on top.

2. Preheat a grill pan or a big nonstick skillet to medium-high heat. Place the sandwiches in the pan with the oil side down. Cover each sandwich in cooking spray and drizzle 1 tsp oil on top. Place a sheet of foil over the sandwiches in the pan and push the sandwiches with a large pan on the foil's top. Roast for a sum of 2 minutes until it's golden brown. Replace the foil and thick skillet after flipping the sandwiches. Prepare for a whole of 2 minutes until it's golden brown. Serve right away.

# Cilantro Flank Steak

Preparation time: 24 mins

Servings: 6

## Ingredients

- One Half flank steak pounds
- Five tsp olive oil (divided)
- One Half tsp Montreal steak seasoning
- One Half cups fresh cilantro leaves, firmly packed
- Two tsp lime juice fresh
- Two garlic cloves (minced)
- Half tsp Salt

## Instructions

1. Drizzle one tablespoon of oil over the steak and season generously.

2. Preheat a cast-iron grill skillet over medium heat and cook the steak for 7 to 9 mins on either side or until desired doneness is reached.

3. In a food processor, combine cilantro, the following three components, and the remaining 4 tbsp oil until smooth. Thinly slice the beef diagonally around the grain. Serve the sauce with the fish.

# Goat Cheese-Stuffed Jalapeños with Ranchero Sauce

Preparation time: 55 mins

Servings: 10

## Ingredients

## Sauce:

- One tsp canola oil
- Two cups onion (vertically sliced)
- Three garlic cloves (minced)
- Water Half cup
- One tsp cumin seeds
- Salt Half tsp
- Half tsp Mexican oregano
- One (15-ounce) tomatoes can, fire-roasted (diced)
- One (8-ounce) tomato sauce can (no-salt-added)

## Jalapeños:

- Cooking spray
- Ten large jalapeño peppers (4 inches long)
- One-Quarter cup (2 ounces) cream cheese block-style fat-free (softened)
- One Quarter tsp salt
- Four ounces goat cheese (softened)
- One garlic clove (minced)
- Ten corn tortillas warmed according to package instruction

## Instructions

1. In a big nonstick pan, heat the oil over medium-high heat to make the sauce. Increase the onion to the frying pan and grill for 3 mins. Add the garlic and simmer for 1 min. Combine 1/2 cup water and the following five components in a mixing bowl (through tomato sauce). Wrap and Cook for 20 mins on low heat. Remove the cover and continue to cook for another 5 minutes.

2. Turn On the oven to 400 degrees Fahrenheit.

3. Preheat a grill pan to medium-high. Oil the plate with nonstick cooking spray. Cook, regularly rotating, for 9 mins or till jalapenos are soft and blackened. Remove the roots, nuts, and membranes from each jalapeno by cutting a lengthwise slit in it.

4. Combine cream cheese and the following three components in a bowl and mix. Load each jalapeno with about a tbsp of the cheese mixture. Arrange the jalapenos on a baking sheet that has been sprayed with cooking mist. Preheat oven to 400°F and bake for 7 mins, or until hot. Toss with tortillas and salsa before serving.

# Grilled Tofu, Bacon, and Avocado Sandwiches

Preparation time: 1 hr. 45 mins

Servings: 4

## Ingredients

- 14 to 16 oz (extra-firm) tofu or block firm
- Two fresh ginger, unpeeled
- Two tsp sugar
- Two pinches pepper
- One Quarter cup soy sauce, low sodium
- One tsp soy sauce dark (black)
- Three tsps. toasted sesame oil
- One tbsp canola oil
- Four ciabatta rolls, split (horizontally)
- Two zucchinis cut longwise into (1/4-in thick slices)
- Three tbsp mayonnaise
- Four tsp Sriracha chili sauce
- Twelve to Fourteen cilantro sprigs (roughly chopped)
- Four slices of cooked bacon halved (crosswise)
- One sliced avocado

## Instructions

1. Cut four 1/2-inch-thick lengthwise slices from the block of tofu. Pack a 9-inch four-sided baking pan halfway with the batter.

2. Using a Microplate, grate the ginger, then press the solids into a fine-mesh sieve into a cup to extract the liquid. In a single cup, weigh two teaspoons ginger juice. Sugar, pepper, soy sauce, sesame oil, and one tablespoon of canola oil are whisked together and poured over tofu. Toss to coat the tofu and set aside for 1 to 2 hours, uncovered, turning halfway through.

3. Gently brush a cast-iron grill pan with more canola oil and flame over medium-high heat before a bead of water evaporates. 2 pieces at a time, sear tofu before grill marks emerge, and tofu quickly releases from skillet, 3 mins per side (reserve marinade). Place on a plate to cool.

4. In a 300° oven, bread cut sides up or toast rolls till crisp, around 15 mins. Meanwhile, toss zucchini with the remaining tofu marinade and grill for 4 minutes per hand or until soft and browned. Save the leftover marinade.

5. Spread 1 tbsp. Mayonnaise on each Half of the bun, then drizzle with 1/2 tbsp. Reserved marinade and 1/2 tbsp. Sriracha. Half of the cilantro can be sprinkled on the bottom roll ends. Toss together the zucchini, avocado, bacon, and tofu. Cover with the rest of the cilantro and the tops of the rolls.

# Quick Panzanella with Chicken

Preparation time: 18 mins

Servings: 4

## Ingredients

- Four chicken breast halves(6-ounce) skinless, boneless
- ¾ tsp salt (divided)
- Half tsp black pepper divided (freshly ground)
- Cooking spray
- Two cups tomato cubed (1-inch)
- Two cups ciabatta bread diced (4 ounces)
- One cup celery lightly sliced (2 stalks)
- Half cup tore basil leaves (fresh)
- Two tsp olive oil, extra-virgin
- Two tsp red wine vinegar
- One small red onion (lightly sliced)
- Half English cucumber, halved longwise and lightly sliced (1 cup)

## Instructions

1. Preheat a grill pan to medium-high. 1/4 tbsp salt and 1/4 tbsp pepper are generously sprinkled over the chicken. Oil the plate with nonstick cooking spray. Cook for 6 mins on either side or until chicken is cooked through. Remove the pan from the heat and chop.

2. Toss the tomato in a wide mixing bowl with the remaining 1/2 tbsp salt and 1/4 tbsp black pepper. Allow for a 5-min rest period. Toss the chicken, bread, and remaining ingredients into the tomato mixture until it is well combined. Serve right away.

## 23. Chicken Fajitas

Preparation time: 1 hr. 32 mins

Servings: 4 servings

### Ingredients

- ¾ cup Mexican beer (dark)
- Two tsp soy sauce, lower sodium
- Two tsp lime juice, fresh
- One tsp canola oil
- One tsp Worcestershire sauce
- Three garlic cloves (crushed)
- One-pound chicken breast halves, skinless, boneless cut across the grain into (1/2-inch-thick strips)
- One cup onion (sliced)
- One orange bell pepper (seeded, sliced)
- One yellow bell pepper (seeded, sliced)
- Cooking spray
- One Quarter tsp salt
- One-Quarter tsp black pepper (freshly ground)
- Eight flour tortillas(6-inch)
- One jalapeño pepper (thinly sliced)
- Salsa (voluntary)
- Sour cream Reduced-fat (voluntary)
- Fresh cilantro leaves (voluntary)

### Instructions

1. In a big blending bowl, mix the first six components and stir well. Placed the chicken in a plastic bag with a zip-top. Fill the bag with 3/4 cup of the beer mixture and close it. Keep the rest of the beer mixture aside. Refrigerate for 1 hour, rotating now and then. Seal a zip-top plastic bag with the onion, bell peppers, and leftover beer mixture. Allow 1 hour to marinate at room temperature.

2. Preheat a grill pan to medium-high. Oil the plate with nonstick cooking spray. Remove the chicken from the container and toss out the marinade. Season the chicken with pepper and salt to taste. Barbecue for 2 mins on either side or until chicken is cooked through. Remove the chicken from the pan and hold it soft. Take the onion or bell peppers out of the bag and throw away the marinade. Cook for 6 minutes, or until the onion mixture is soft, rotating after 3 mins. If required, toast tortillas in a skillet. Put two tortillas on each of four plates and divide the chicken mixture evenly among them. Distribute the onion mixture evenly among the servings. Serve garnished with jalapeno strips. If needed, top with lettuce, sour cream, and cilantro.

# Grilled Lobster Tails

Preparation time: 25 mins

servings: 6

## Ingredients

- Six lobster tails 8-10 ounces each (thawed & frozen)
- 3/4 cup olive oil
- Three tbsps. (minced) fresh chives
- Three garlic cloves (minced)
- Half tsp salt
- Half tsp pepper

## Instructions

1. Cut 3 - 4 (lengthwise) slits in the underside of the tail with "scissors" to loosen the shell moderately. Using scissors, cut the top of the lobster shell (lengthwise) down the middle, leaving the tail fin intact. Cut the shell at the base of the tail fin at such an "angle" away from the center of the tail. Remove the meat from the body, leaving the (fin) end attached; raise the meat & place it on top of the shell.

2. Mix the remaining ingredients in a small bowl and spoon over the lobster meat. Put it in the fridge for 20 mins after covering.

3. Arrange lobster tails on grill rack, meat side up. Cover &cook for 10-12 mins over medium heat or till the meat is opaque.

# Grilled Chicken Salad with Blueberry Vinaigrette

Preparation time: 30 mins

servings: 4

## Ingredients

- Two chicken boneless (skinless) breast halves, about six ounces each
- one tbsp olive oil
- one garlic clove (minced)
- 1/4 tsp salt
- 1/4 tsp pepper
- 1/4 cup, olive oil
- 1/4 cup, blueberry preserves
- Two tbsp of balsamic vinegar
- Two tbsp of maple syrup
- 1/4 tsp, ground mustard
- 1/8 tsp, salt
- Dash pepper
- One package, salad greens (of about ten ounces)
- One cup, blueberries, fresh
- Half cup, mandarin oranges (canned)
- One cup, goat cheese (crumbled)

## Instructions

1. Toss the chicken with garlic, oil, salt n pepper; chill for 30 mins, wrapped. Whisk together the vinaigrette ingredients in a small bowl; cover & chill it before ready to use.
2. Cover &grill chicken for about 5-7 mins per side over medium heat before a thermometer reads 165°. Allow for a 5 min rest before slicing.
3. Toss greens with blueberries, chicken, & mandarin oranges on a serving tray. Re-whisk the vinaigrette & drizzle it over the salad. Place a slice of cheese on top.

# Grilled Steak Bruschetta Salad for 2

Preparation time: 25 mins

servings: 2

## Ingredients

- Half lb. of beef (tenderloin) steaks, one inch thick
- 1/4 tsp salt
- 1/8 tsp pepper
- Two slices of "Italian" bread (Half inch thick)
- One cup arugula, fresh / baby spinach, fresh
- 1/3 cup, jarred / bruschetta topping (prepared)
- 1/3 cup "blue cheese" salad dressing

## Instructions

1. Season all sides of the steaks with salt n pepper. 6-8 mins on either hand, sealed over medium heat before meat achieves desired doneness (a thermometer can read 135° for medium-rare, 140° for medium, and 145° for medium-well). Allow for a 5 mins rest period.

2. Toast the bread, wrapped, for 1-2 mins on either side; switch to salad plates.

3. Thinly slice the steak and put it on top of the bread. Arugula & bruschetta (topping) go on top. Firecracker drizzling

# Grilled Salmon

Preparation time: 25 mins

servings: 4

## Ingredients

- Two tbsp, balsamic vinegar
- Two tbsp, reduced-sodium soy sauce
- One green onion (thinly sliced)
- One tbsp, olive oil
- One tbsp, maple syrup
- Two, garlic cloves (minced)
- One tsp, ground ginger
- One tsp red pepper flakes (crushed)
- Half tsp sesame oil
- 1/4 tsp salt
- Four salmon fillets, Six ounces each.

## Instructions

1. Combine the very first Ten ingredients in a shallow mixing cup. Fill a big resealable plastic bag with 1/4 cup marinade. Seal the bag & turn to coat the salmon. Put it in the fridge for about 30 mins before serving. Cover & keep the remaining marinade refrigerated.

2. Drain the salmon, reserving the marinade in the bag. Place the salmon on the oiled grill rack, skin side down. Cover & grill over high heat for about 5-10 mins, or broil three to four inches from the heat about 5-10 mins, till the fish flakes (easily) with a fork, basting regularly with leftover marinade.

# Grilled Broccoli

Preparation time: 15 mins

servings: 6

## Ingredients

- Six cups, broccoli spears (fresh)
- Two tbsp plus half tsp lemon juice
- Two tbsp olive oil
- 1/4 tsp salt
- 1/4 tsp pepper
- 3/4 cup, Parmesan cheese (grated)
- Optional - lemon slices (Grilled) & red pepper flakes

## Instructions

1. In a big mixing bowl, position the broccoli. Toss broccoli with lemon juice, grease, salt, and pepper, and toss to cover. Allow for 30 minutes of resting time.

2. Toss the broccoli and rinse it, discarding the marinade. In the small shallow dish, position the cheese. Toss in a few slices of broccoli at a time to coat.

3. Use a drip pan to prepare the grill for indirect heat. On a greased grill grate, arrange broccoli over the drip pan. Cover & grill for about 8-10 mins on either side over indirect medium heat or till the crisp tender. Garnish it with some grilled lemon slices & red pepper flakes, if desired.

# Honey Thyme Grilled Chicken

Preparation time: 25 mins

servings: 4

## Ingredients

- 1/4 cup, olive oil
- 1/4 cup, honey
- One garlic clove (minced)
- Eight chicken drumsticks, about two lbs.
- One tsp (dried) thyme
- 3/4 tsp, salt
- 1/4 tsp, pepper

## Instructions

1. In the small cup, whisk together the oil, butter, and garlic. Season the drumsticks with salt and pepper.

2. Brush a light coating of cooking oil on the grill rack. Cover and grill chicken over medium heat for 15-20 mins, till a thermometer reaches 170°-175° F, turning & brushing regularly.

# Grilled Eggplant Parmesan Stacks

Preparation time: 25 mins

servings: 4

## Ingredients

- One big eggplant of about two lbs.
- Half tsp, salt
- One tbsp, olive oil
- Half tsp, pepper
- One log of (fresh) mozzarella cheese (one lb.), cut in 16 slices
- One big tomato (cut in eight slices)
- Half cup, Parmesan cheese (shredded)
- fresh basil/parsley (Chopped)

## Instructions

1. Trim the ends of the eggplant & cut it into eight slices crosswise. Season with salt and set aside for five min.

2. Pat the eggplant (dry) with "paper towels" before brushing it with oil & seasoning it with pepper on both sides. Cover & grill for 4-6 mins on each side on medium heat, or till tender. Remove the grill from the heat.

3. Arrange onion, mozzarella, & Parmesan cheese on top of the eggplant. Cover & cook for another 1-2 mins, or before the cheese starts to melt. In the last 5 mins, drizzle with honey mixture generously.

# Lime and Garlic Grilled Pork Chops

Preparation time: 25 mins

servings: 6

## Ingredients

- one can of "frozen" limeade concentrate (about 12 ounces), thawed

- 1/4 cup, white vinegar

- two tbsp, fresh cilantro (minced)

- five garlic cloves (minced)

- one tbsp, fresh ginger root (minced)

- one tsp salt

- one tsp pepper

- four drops of some 'jalapeno' pepper sauce

- six bone-in pork (chops), about 8 ounces each

- optional - fresh cilantro (Chopped)

## Instructions

1. Combine the very first Eight ingredients in a shallow mixing cup. Add 1-1/4 cup marinade Toss in the pork & turn to coat. Put it in the fridge for about 4 hrs. after covering. Refrigerate the leftover marinade for basting.

2. Drain the pork and toss out the marinade. Grill chops, covered, for 4-6 minutes on either side or until a thermometer reads 160° on a finely oiled rack on the medium heat or broil Four inches from the heat, basting regularly with reserved marinade. Garnish with chopped cilantro if necessary.

# Grilled Tilapia with Mango

Preparation time: 20 mins

servings: 4

## Ingredients

- four tilapia fillets (6 ounces each)
- one tbsp, olive oil
- half tsp, salt
- half tsp, dill weed
- 1/4 tsp, pepper
- one tbsp Parmesan cheese (grated)
- one medium lemon (sliced)
- one medium-sized mango (peeled & thinly sliced)

## Instructions

1. Drizzle oil over the fillets &season with salt, dill, & pepper.

2. Cook tilapia for 5 minutes on a slightly greased rack on medium heat, sealed. Turn the tilapia and serve with cheese, ginger, & mango on top. Grill for an additional 4-6 mins, or before the fish flakes quickly with a fork.

# Grilled Pork Burgers

Preparation time: 25 mins

servings: 6

## Ingredients

- One big egg (lightly beaten)
- 3/4 cup, soft breadcrumbs
- 3/4 cup, Parmesan cheese (grated)
- One tbsp parsley flakes (dried)
- Two tsps. dried basil
- Half tsp, salt
- Half tsp, garlic powder
- 1/4 tsp, pepper
- Two lbs., ground pork
- Six hamburger buns (split)
- Optional - Sliced tomato, Lettuce leaves & sweet onion

## Instructions

1. Add the very first 8 ingredients in a big mixing bowl. Pork should be crumbled over the mixture & mix thoroughly. Create six patties out of the mixture.

2. Cover and grill burgers for about 4-5 min on either side over medium heat or until the thermometer reaches 160° F.

3. Toss on lettuce, tomato, & onion, if necessary, then serve on buns.

# Grilled Steak and Mushroom Salad

Preparation time: 30 mins

servings: 6

## Ingredients

- Six tbsp olive oil (divided)
- Two tbsp Dijon mustard, (divided)
- Half tsp, salt
- 1/4 tsp, pepper
- One beef top (sirloin) steak, 1-1/2 lbs.
- 1 lb. mushrooms (sliced & fresh)
- 1/4 cup, red wine vinegar
- One medium (bunch) romaine, torn

## Instructions

1. Add 1 tbsp oil, 1 tbsp mustard, salt, & pepper in a small bowl; set aside.

2. Cover & grill the steak for 4 mins over medium-high heat. Turn & coat it with the mustard mixture. Grill for another 4 mins, or till the meat achieves desired doneness (a thermometer can read 135° for medium-rare, 140° for medium, and 145° for medium-well).

3. Meanwhile, fry the mushrooms in 1 tbsp oil in a big skillet until tender. Combine the vinegar, remaining oil, & mustard in a mixing cup.

4. Thinly slice the steak against the grain & toss it into the mushroom mixture.

# Grilled Caprese Quesadillas

Preparation time: 20 mins

servings: 2

## Ingredients

- Four wheat tortillas (8 inches)
- Six ounces mozzarella cheese (fresh &sliced)
- Two medium tomatoes (sliced & patted dry)
- 1/3 cup, julienned basil (fresh)
- 1/4 cup, pitted Greek olives (chopped)
- Pepper (freshly ground) to taste

## Instructions

1. Spread cheese & tomatoes on half of each tortilla; top with basil, olives, & pepper to taste. To close the tortillas, fold them in half.

2. Grill, sealed, for 2-3 minutes per side on medium-high heat till slightly browned & cheese is melted.

# Grilled Pineapple Chicken

Preparation time: 20 mins

servings: 4

## Ingredients

- 1/4 cup, pineapple juice (unsweetened)
- Two tbsp, sherry
- Two tbsp, soy sauce
- 1/4 tsp, ground ginger
- Dash salt
- Dash pepper
- Four chicken boneless (skinless) breast, halves (six ounces)
- Optional - Grilled pineapple & green onions (sliced)

## Instructions

1. Combine the very first 6 ingredients in a big mixing bowl; add the chicken & toss to cover. Put it in the fridge for 1-2 hrs., covered.

2. Drain the marinade and toss it out. Cover & grill chicken for about 5-7 mins on each side over medium heat or broil 4 inches from the heat till a meat thermometer reaches 165° F. Serve it with (grilled) pineapple & (sliced) green onions if desired.

# Grilled Angel Food Cake with Fruit Salsa

Preparation time: 15 mins

servings: 6

## Ingredients

- half cup of each fresh blueberry, raspberries & strawberries (Chopped)
- one medium kiwifruit (peeled & chopped)
- two tbsps. sugar
- one tbsp lime juice
- one (loaf-shaped) angel food cake (of about 10-1/2 ounces)
- optional - Whipped topping

## Instructions

1. Mix the bananas, kiwi, sugar, & lime juice in a small cup. Grill cake cut side down for 1-3 min on the medium heat or broil Four inches from heat until well browned. Round the cake into slices. Serve it with some fruit salsa & whipped topping, if needed.

# Summer Turkey Kabobs

Preparation time: 30 mins

servings: 6

## Ingredients

- Two, "yellow summer squash," small
- Two, small zucchinis
- One can of whole drained potatoes (15 ounces)
- Two tbsp olive oil
- One package "turkey" breast tenderloins (20 ounces)
- Half tsp, pepper
- 1/4 tsp salt
- One package (torn mixed) salad greens (5 ounces)
- One cup, salad croutons
- Half cup, red wine vinaigrette

## Instructions

1. Cut yellow squash & zucchini crosswise into 1" slices after trimming the ends. In a big mixing dish, combine the slices & potatoes. Toss the mixture in the oil to coat it.

2. Cut the "turkey" into 24 cubes & combine it with the vegetables. Season with pepper n salt & toss once more.

3. Thread turkey balls, squash, zucchini, & potatoes alternately on six soaked wooden or metal skewers. Cover & cook over medium heat, stirring regularly, for 12-15 minutes, or till the "turkey" is no longer pink & vegetables are crisp-tender. Serve with croutons on a bed of leaves. Drizzle vinaigrette on top.

# Spice-Rubbed Chicken Thighs

Preparation time: 20 mins

servings: 6

## Ingredients

- One tsp, salt
- One tsp, garlic powder
- One tsp, onion powder
- One tsp, dried oregano
- Half tsp, ground turmeric
- Half tsp, paprika
- 1/4 tsp, chili powder
- 1/4 tsp, pepper
- Six boneless chicken (skinless) thighs (of about Half lbs.)

## Instructions

1. Combine the very first 8 ingredients in a shallow mixing cup. Sprinkle all sides of the chicken with the seasoning.

2. Grill the chicken (covered) on medium heat or broil Four inches from heat till a thermometer reaches 170°, 6-8 mins on every side, on a (finely greased) grill rack.

# Fajita in a Bowl

Preparation time: 30 mins

servings: 4

## Ingredients

- One tbsp brown sugar
- One tbsp chili powder
- Half tsp of salt
- One beef steak (flank) of 1 lb.
- Twelve sweet peppers (miniature), halved & seeded
- One red onion (medium), cut in some thin wedges
- Two cups, cherry tomatoes
- Two sweet corn (medium), with husks, removed
- Twelve cups of salad greens (torn mixed)
- One cup, cilantro leaves (fresh)
- Half cup lime vinaigrette (reduced & fat)

## Optional ingredients:

lime wedges, Cotija cheese & tortillas

## Instructions

1. Combine chili powder, brown sugar, & salt in a small cup. Rub all the sides of the steak with the rub.

2. Put peppers & onion on the grilling grid & cook it over medium heat on a grill rack. 9-11 mins, sealed, till it gets crisp-tender, stirring occasionally; add the tomatoes in the last Two mins of cooking. Remove the grill from the heat.

3. Close the lid & place the steak & corn direct on the grill grate. 8-10 mins on every side, or till the thermometer reads 135° F for medium-rare; 10-12 mins on every side, or till mildly burnt, turning slightly.

4. Split the cilantro & greens into four bowls. Corn should be cut from the cobs, & steak should be thinly sliced around the grain & placed in cups. Drizzle with vinaigrette and finish with vegetables. Serve with cheese, mint, and tortillas if desired.

# Oktoberfest Brats with Mustard Sauce

Preparation time: 20 mins

servings: 4

## Ingredients

- 1/3 cup, cream (half-n-half)
- Two tbsps. Mustard (stone-ground)
- Half tsp onion (dried & minced)
- 1/4 tsp, pepper
- Dash paprika
- Four bratwurst links (fully cooked), about Twelve ounces
- One can of sauerkraut (warmed, rinsed & drained), 14 ounces

## Instructions

1. To make the sauce, combine the first 5 ingredients. Using the 4 soaked/metal wooden skewers, string each bratwurst into thirds.

2. Cover & grill brats over medium heat for 7-10 mins, rotating regularly, till it gets golden brown & cooked through. Serve with sauce & sauerkraut on the side.

# Grilled Eggplant Sandwiches

Preparation time: 25 mins

servings: 2

## Ingredients

- 2 tbsps. olive oil

- One garlic clove (minced)

- Two ciabatta rolls (split)

- Four slices of eggplant of about half an inch thick

- One heirloom tomato (medium), cut in half an inch slices

- 1/4 tsp salt

- 1/8 tsp pepper

- Two ounces goat cheese (fresh & softened)

- Six basil leaves (fresh)

## Instructions

1. Combine the oil & garlic, then rub it on the cut sides of the rolls as well as all sides of the vegetables. Season the vegetables with some salt n pepper.

2. Cover & grill eggplant over medium heat till tender, around 4-5 mins per side. Cover & grill tomato for about 1-2 mins per hand, till it gets finely browned. Grill rolls for 1-2 mins, cut the side down, till toasted.

3. Spread goat cheese on the bottoms of the rolls. Close sandwiches & top with eggplant, spinach, & tomato.

# Grilled Stone Fruits with Balsamic Syrup

Preparation time: 20 mins

servings: 4

## Ingredients

- Half cup, balsamic vinegar

- Two tbsps., brown sugar

- Two medium peaches (peeled & halved)

- Two medium nectarines (peeled & halved)

- Two medium plums (peeled & halved)

## Instructions

1. Mix vinegar & brown sugar in a shallow saucepan. Bring it to a boil, then simmer till the liquid has been reduced by half.

2. Grill nectarines, peaches, & plums, covered over the medium heat or broil Four in. from heat till soft, 3-4 mins on either side, on a well-oiled grill rack.

3. Cut the fruits into slices & place them on a serving tray. Drizzle the sauce on top.

# Chicken Caesar Pitas

Preparation time: 30 mins

servings: 4

## Ingredients

- 3/4 tsp, dried oregano
- Half tsp dried basil
- 1/4 tsp, onion powder
- 1/4 tsp, paprika
- 1/8 tsp, dried mint
- One lb. chicken skinless breasts (boneless)
- Two cups, torn romaine
- One cup, brown rice
- Half cup, Caesar vinaigrette (reduced fat)
- Eight wheat pita pocket halves, whole

## Instructions

1. Combine the very first 5 ingredients in the "spice grinder" or in a mortar & pestle; grind till the mixture is perfect. Rub all over the chicken.

2. On a greased grill, cook the chicken for about 4-5 mins on either side, covered, over the medium heat or "broil" 4 inches, from the heat, or till the thermometer measures 170°, F. Break into 1/2-inch slices till it gets cool enough to touch. Chill in the fridge.

3. Combine the romaine, chicken, & rice in the big mixing dish. Drizzle the vinaigrette over the salad & toss to coat. Pitas are a great way to serve this dish.

# Grilled Lemon-Dill Shrimp

Preparation time: 30 mins

servings: 4

## Ingredients

- 1/4 cup, olive oil
- One tbsp, lemon juice
- Two tsps., dill weed
- Two garlic cloves (minced)
- 3/4 tsp salt
- Half tsp, pepper
- One lb. shrimp (uncooked), peeled & deveined

## Instructions

1. In a big mixing bowl, mix the first Six ingredients together till well combined. Set aside Three tbsp marinade for basting. Toss their shrimp in the residual marinade to coat. Refrigerate for 15 mins, sealed.

2. Rinse the shrimp & remove the marinade. 4 or maybe 8 metal / soaked wooden skewers, threaded with shrimp Grill 2-4 mins on each foot, sealed, on medium heat or broil 4 inches from heat, basting with the (reserved) marinade in the last min of cooking.

# Grilled Chicken and Mango Skewers

Preparation time: 30 mins

servings: 4

## Ingredients

- Three ears sweet corn (medium)
- One tbsp butter
- 1/3 cup plus Three tbsps. green onions (sliced & divided)
- One lb. chicken skinless breasts (boneless), cut in one-inch cubes
- Half tsp salt
- 1/4 tsp pepper
- One medium mango (peeled & cut in one-inch cubes)
- 1 tbsp olive oil (extra-virgin)
- optional - Lime wedges

## Instructions

1. Remove the cobs of corn from the cobs. Heat butter in a large skillet over medium-high heat and cook cut corn till gets crisp-tender, around 5 mins. Mix in green onions (1/3 cup), chopped. Keep it warm.

2. Season the chicken with salt n pepper before serving. Thread chicken & mango alternately onto Four metal / soaked wooden skewers. Apply some oil to the brush.

3. Grill, protected, on medium heat, or broil four inches from heat for about 10-12 mins, rotating periodically, till the chicken is no longer "pink." Serve it with the corn mixture & the (remaining) green onions on top. Serve it with lime wedges if needed.

# Berried Treasure Angel Food Cake

Preparation time: 25 mins

servings: 4

## Ingredients

- Eight slices of food cake, the angel (1-1/2 inches thick)
- 1/4 cup, butter (softened)
- Half cup of whipping cream (Heavy)
- 1/4 tsp, almond extract
- 1/4 cup, almond cake & pastry filling
- Half cup of fresh blueberries
- Half cup of fresh raspberries
- Half cup of fresh strawberries (sliced)
- 1/4 cup, mixed nuts (coarsely chopped)
- Confectioners' sugar

## Instructions

1. Cut out centers of half of "cake slices" with a 1-1/2-inch round cookie cutter (take out the removed cake or set aside for another use). Brush all sides of the cake slices with sugar. Grill 1-2 mins on either foot, sealed, on medium heat, or broil four inches from heat till it gets toasted.

2. In a shallow mixing cup, beat milk till it thickens. Add the extract & continue to beat till it is in soft peaks form.

3. To serve, place one solid & one (cutout) slice of the cake on every desert pan, with the outside ends on (opposite) sides for an equal thickness. Cover holes with almond filling, & finish with some whipped cream, fruit, & nuts. Confectioners' sugar is sprinkled on top.

# Cilantro Lime Shrimp

Preparation time: 30 mins

servings: 4

## Ingredients

- 1/3 cup, fresh cilantro (chopped)
- Half tsp lime zest (grated)
- 1/3 cup, lime juice
- One jalapeno pepper (seeded & minced)
- Two tbsp olive oil
- Three garlic cloves (minced)
- 1/4 tsp salt
- 1/4 tsp ground cumin
- 1/4 tsp pepper
- One lb. shrimp (uncooked) 16-20 per pound, peeled & deveined
- Lime slices

## Instructions

1. Combine the very first nine ingredients & toss it with the shrimp. Place it for 15 mins.

2. Thread Four soaked /metal, wooden skewers with shrimp & lime slices. Cover & grill over medium heat for 2-4 mins per hand, or till the shrimp turn yellow.

# Easy Grilled Squash

Preparation time: 20 mins

servings: 4

## Ingredients

- Three tbsp olive oil
- Two garlic cloves (minced)
- 1/4 tsp salt
- 1/4 tsp pepper
- One butternut squash, small (peeled & cut in half-inch slices lengthwise)

## Instructions

1. Mix the oil, garlic, salt, n pepper in a shallow cup. Brush the squash slices with the oil.

2. Cover & grill squash for about 4-5 mins on either side on medium heat / broil four inches from the heat till tender.

# Grilled Sausage-Basil Pizzas

Preparation time: 30 mins

servings: 4

## Ingredients

- Four sausage links, Italian (Four ounces each)
- Four naan flatbreads/pita breads, whole
- 1/4 cup, olive oil
- One cup, tomato (basil) pasta sauce
- Two cups, (part-skim) mozzarella cheese, shredded
- Half cup Parmesan cheese (grated)
- Half cup fresh basil (thinly sliced)

## Instructions

1. Cook sausages (covered) on medium heat for about 10-12 mins, till a thermometer measures 160° F. Break it in 1/4-inch-thick slices.

2. Brush flatbreads with oil on both ends. Cover flatbreads &grill over medium heat for 2-3 minutes, or till the bottoms are slightly browned.

3. Take the grill off the sun. Sauce, bacon, cheeses, & basil are layered on grilled ends. Return to the grill & cook for another 2-3 mins, sealed, till the cheese has melted.

# Chicken with Peach-Cucumber Salsa

Preparation time: 25 mins

servings: 4

## Ingredients

- Half cup fresh peaches (peeled)
- 3/4 cup cucumber (chopped)
- Four tbsps. peach preserves (divided)
- Three tbsps. red onion (finely chopped)
- One tsp fresh mint (minced)
- 3/4 tsp salt (divided)
- Four chicken boneless (skinless) breast 'halves (6 ounces each)
- 1/4 tsp pepper

## Instructions

1. To make the salsa, add peaches, cucumber, two tsp preserves, mint, onion, &1/4 tsp salt in a small mixing bowl.

2. Season the chicken with the (remaining) salt n pepper. Grill chicken for about 5 mins, wrapped, on a lightly greased grill grate over medium heat. Turn; cook for another 7-9 minutes, till a thermometer reaches 165° F, brushing tops with (remaining) preserves if needed. Serve with a side of salsa.

# Grilled Zucchini with Onions

Preparation time: 20 mins

servings: 4

**Ingredients**

- Six small zucchinis (halved lengthwise)

- Four tsp olive oil (divided)

- Two green onions (thinly sliced)

- 2 tbsp lemon juice

- Half tsp salt.

- 1/8 tsp red pepper flakes (crushed)

Instructions

1. Drizzle 2 tsp oil across zucchini. Grill, sealed, about 8-10 mins or till tender, rotating once, over medium fire.

2. Transfer to a big mixing cup. Toss in the lemon juice, green onions, salt n pepper flakes, as well as the remaining oil.

# Fruit-Glazed Pork Chops

Preparation time: 20 mins

servings: 6

## Ingredients

- 1/3 cup (smoke-flavored) barbecue sauce, hickory.
- Half cup, apricot/peach preserves
- One tbsp, corn syrup
- One tsp mustard, prepared
- 1/4 tsp ground cloves
- Six bone-in pork loin (chops), about ¾" thick & Eight ounces each)
- Half tsp, salt
- Half tsp, pepper

## Instructions

1. Mix the preserves, barbecue sauce, mustard, corn syrup, & cloves in a small bowl; set aside.

2. Season pork chops liberally with salt n pepper. Grill chops (covered), about 4-5 mins on either side till the thermometer reads 145° F on a slightly oiled grill /broil four to five inches from the sun, basting regularly with sauce mixture. Allow 5 mins for the meat to rest before eating.

# Conclusion

Hopefully, after interpreting this recipe book, you realized that this book is excellent for getting to know regarding the indoor grilling & new recipes to try & make with the indoor grill & believe it, these serving dishes are delicious to eat. This guide includes several recipes & techniques to do with your indoor grill, & it covers more than 100 recipes with several combinations.

Introduction to Indoor grilling, top indoor grill models, barbequing vs grilling, the key difference between both words, and which one is better. It includes pork, seafood, chicken, vegetables, desserts, beef, lamb, and many different recipes. This recipe book covers nearly all facets, and after reading this book, you would likely turn out to be a specialist without getting any help from experts & will also be able to guide the ones who are new to indoor grilling.

All recipes include preparation time, servings, ingredients, and brief instructions, helping you understand the recipes easily. It allows you to become an expert chef of indoor grilling after trying different recipes of different categories. The exciting thing is that all recipes are easy to make. Only a few of them are somehow tricky but can be made.

Printed in Great Britain
by Amazon

81737827R00079